R Lespinasse

Notes on Niagara

R Lespinasse

Notes on Niagara

ISBN/EAN: 9783743333963

Manufactured in Europe, USA, Canada, Australia, Japa

Cover: Foto ©ninafisch / pixelio.de

Manufactured and distributed by brebook publishing software (www.brebook.com)

R Lespinasse

Notes on Niagara

NOTES
ON
NIAGARA

EDITED BY
R. LESPINASSE.

ILLUSTRATED BY PROMINENT ARTISTS.

CHICAGO
R. LESPINASSE, PUBLISHER.
1884.

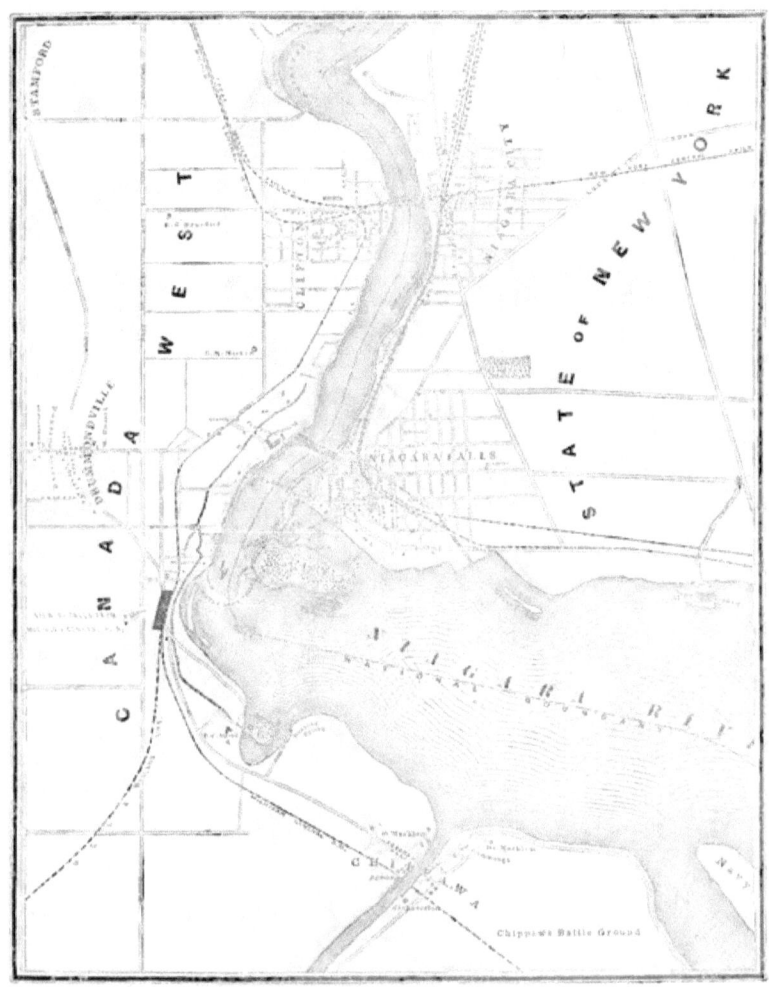

MAP OF THE VICINITY OF NIAGARA FALLS.

PREFACE.

RELYING upon mere words to make the people familiar with a most superb creation of Nature, and describe impressions of the grandeur and sublimity of the Falls of Niagara, would prove a futile attempt.

The artist's pencil alone can convey a faint idea of the more salient features of Niagara, and must of necessity supplement the most gorgeous and brilliant description. Even at its best it proves inadequate to express that in which lies its deepest charm—everlasting motion and perpetual change, conjoined with an all-pervading sense of unity.

Eyes, mind and heart go in unison; writing is useless, art is powerless, to depict the weird majesty of the scene.

We have endeavored to make the work beautiful and attractive, gathering in one volume the best words of eloquent pens and happiest conceptions of thorough artists.

How well we have succeeded in attaining our aim remains for the reader to determine.

PUBLISHER'S NOTE.

REFERENCE, in the course of this volume, to numerous prominent authors, has contributed largely to the spicy variations and interesting features of our text. As a matter of justice, as well as courtesy, the publishers of these various works deserve special mention at our hands.

The fac-simile of engravings inserted in our pages, illustrate, mostly, familiar points and landmarks of earlier days, now obliterated.

Excerpts are from the following works:

GEORGE HOUGHTON—NIAGARA AND OTHER POEMS.
    Houghton, Mifflin & Co., Publishers, Boston, Mass.
LADY DUFFUS HARDY—THROUGH CITIES AND PRAIRIE LANDS.
    Belford, Clarke & Co., Publishers, Chicago, Ill., 1882.
CHARLES DICKENS—AMERICAN NOTES.
N. P. WILLIS—AMERICAN SCENERY.
    Geo. Virtue, Publisher, London, 1839.
GEORGE W. HOLLEY—THE FALLS OF NIAGARA.
    A. C. Armstrong & Son., Publishers, New York, 1883.
H. T. ALLEN—ILLUSTRATED GUIDE TO NIAGARA.
    H. T. Allen, Publisher, Niagara Falls, N. Y., 1881.
JACQUES OFFENBACH—OFFENBACH IN AMERICA.
    G. W. Carleton & Co., Publishers, New York, 1877.
MRS. SIGOURNEY—SCENES IN MY NATIVE LAND.
C. H. A. BULKLEY—NIAGARA—A POEM.
    Leavitt, Trow & Co., Publishers, New York, 1848.
J. B. HARRISON—LETTERS ON THE CONDITION OF NIAGARA FALLS.
    Franklin Falls, N. H., 1882.
JOHN M. DUNCAN—TRAVELS THROUGH PART OF THE UNITED STATES AND CANADA.
    University Press, Glasgow, 1818.
CAPT. BASIL HALL—TRAVELS IN NORTH AMERICA.
    Robert Cadell, Publisher, Edinburgh, 1828.
JAMES STUART—THREE YEARS IN NORTH AMERICA.
    London Edition, 1834.
CHAS. AUGUSTUS MURRAY—TRAVELS IN NORTH AMERICA.
    Harper & Bros., Publishers, New York, 1839.
J. S. BUCKINGHAM—AMERICA—HISTORICAL, STATISTIC AND DESCRIPTIVE.
    Harper & Bros., Publishers, New York, 1841.
CHARLES LYELL—TRAVELS IN NORTH AMERICA.
    Wiley & Putnam, Publishers, New York, 1845.
COL. P. DONAN—Pamphlet on MACKINAC ISLAND.
    Chicago, Ill., 1883.

CONTENTS

	PAGE
PREFACE,	7
PUBLISHER'S NOTE,	8
LIST OF ILLUSTRATIONS,	13
PHILOSOPHICAL REFLECTIONS — Col. P. Donan,	16
BIRD'S EYE VIEW OF NIAGARA FALLS,	17
EARLY GLIMPSES,	19
LA SALLE'S EXPLORATIONS,	20
HENNEPIN'S ACCOUNT,	21
BARON LA HONTAINE,	25
FIGURES BY CHARLEVOIX,	25
EIGHTEENTH CENTURY NOTES — Peter Kalm,	27
L'Abbe Piequet,	28
Weld's Visit,	28
INDIAN LEGENDS,	30
RED JACKET,	32
BELOW THE GREAT FALL — John M. Duncan,	34
CREATION'S PRIDE — Wilhelm Meister,	36
THE OLD FERRY LANDING — American Side,	37
AMERICAN RAPIDS — N. P. Willis,	38
NIAGARA — Translated by Wm. Cullen Bryant,	39
ALBUM SKETCH — Col. Porter,	40
BEHIND THE SHEET OF WATER — Chas. A. Murray,	42
CAPTAIN HALL'S NARRATIVE — On Goat Island,	43
Neighborhood Scenery,	44
First Goat Island Bridge,	44
Crossing to Canada,	46
IMPRESSIONS — James Stuart,	47
THE HORSE-SHOE FALL — N. P. Willis,	48
A THRILLING ESCAPE — Wm. Hosea Ballou,	50
TABLE ROCK,	52
THE HERMIT OF THE FALLS — Mrs. Sigourney,	55
THE RAMBLER — Chas. Jos. Latrobe,	60
A SYNCOPE OF THE WATERS — Geo. W. Holley,	66
THE NIAGARA RIVER,	68
DICKEN'S NOTES,	72

	PAGE
BURNING OF THE CAROLINE — H. T. Allen,	75
HOW TO SEE THE CATARACT — J. B. Harrison,	78
Existing Conditions,	78
Four Separate Waterfalls,	78
Framework of Foliage,	80
Why Some Persons are Disappointed,	81
Misused Opportunities,	82
Prospect Park,	84
Goat Island,	85
The Rapids,	86
A LAST LOOK — J. S. Buckingham,	88
THE RAPIDS AND GORGE — George Houghton,	89
THE MAID OF THE MIST — Geo. W. Holley,	91
THE CATARACT,	94
THE NEW SUSPENSION BRIDGE,	96
FROM CITY TO CATARACT — Lady Duffus Hardy,	99
NIAGARA FALLS FROM CANADA — General View,	100
Table Rock,	100
The Rapids,	101
Clark Hill Islands,	102
The Burning Spring,	102
Above the Falls,	104
Lundy's Lane,	106
Whirlpool Rapids,	106
The Whirlpool,	106
THE ROAR OF THE FALLS,	107
DEPTHS OF NIAGARA'S CANYON — W. H. Ballou,	108
IN WINTER,	110
Ice Mound,	112
A BOLD SWIM,	113
Captain Webb in the Rapids,	114
Theories as to Manner of Death,	115
INTERNATIONAL PARK PROJECT,	118
A Plea for Preservation — J. B. Harrison,	119
ACROSS NIAGARA RIVER,	122
Progress of the Work,	124
OFFENBACH ON NIAGARA,	128
SPECULATIONS OF THE SCIENTISTS:	
RETROCESSION OF THE FALLS — Sir Charles Lyell,	129
Reduced Height,	130
Recent Proofs of Erosion,	130
Remnants of an old River Bed,	131
The Devil's Hole,	133
Recession,	133
Future Retrocession,	134
Origin of the Falls,	135
Lapse of Time,	136
PAST AND FUTURE — Prof. Tyndall,	140
Effects of the Sand Blast,	140
Erosive Power of Rivers,	141
Origin and Progress of the Cataract,	142
In the Past,	142

CONTENTS—CONTINUED.

	PAGE.
PAST AND FUTURE — Erosive Power of the Horse-Shoe Fall,	134
The Future,	144
GRATUITOUS ASSERTIONS — J. M. Duncan,	146
NIAGARA FALLS, ONTARIO,	150
VILLAGE OF NIAGARA FALLS, N. Y.,	151
The Hackman,	152
RETROSPECT — L. Deville,	154
BRIEF GUIDE TO NIAGARA FALLS AND VICINITY,	155
AGREEMENTS,	160

LIST OF ILLUSTRATIONS.

SUBJECT.	ARTIST.	PAGE.
Niagara,	GUSTAVE DORÉ,	Frontispiece
Map of the Vicinity of Niagara Falls,	——	5
A Sweet Singer,	——	6
Blooming Cactuses,	——	12
A Tony Tourist,	FRANK R. GREEN,	16
Bird's Eye View from Upper Rapids to the Whirlpool,	F. C. BROMLEY,	17
Indian Head,	F. R. GREEN,	19
Stone Towers of Fort Frontenac in 1676,	CHAS. GRAHAM,	20
La Salle's Fort and Palisades, 1678,	F. C. BROMLEY,	20
Hennepin's View (Fac-simile),	FATHER HENNEPIN,	23
General View in 1796 (Fac-simile),	J. WELD,	26
Flying Ducks,	F. C. BROMLEY,	28
Distant View in 1884,	CHAS. VOLKMAR,	29
From Far Scattered Camps,	F. E. LUMIS,	30
The Indian's Sacrifice to Niagara's God's,	CHAS. VOLKMAR,	31
The House of Red Jacket,	C. GRAHAM,	32
Portrait of Red Jacket (Fac-simile),	WEIR,	33
Horse-Shoe Falls from below,	F. C. BROMLEY,	35
Creation's Pride (Pen Text),	F. C. BROMLEY,	36
The Old Ferry Landing (Fac-simile),	W. H. BARTLETT,	37
"Thy Forest Pines are Fittest Coronal,"	FRANK R. GREEN,	39
Portrait of Wm. Cullen Bryant,	FRANK R. GREEN,	39
The Chief, the Soldier of the Sword, the Soldier of the Cross,	CHAS. VOLKMAR,	41
Under Table Rock in 1835 (Fac-simile),	W. H. BARTLETT,	42
Viewing the Falls,	F. R. GREEN,	43
On Goat Island,	ALFRED TRUMBLE,	44
View from Prospect Point,	A. MIES,	45
Brock's Monument and Obelisk,	F. C. BROMLEY,	46

LIST OF ILLUSTRATIONS.—Continued.

SUBJECT.	ARTIST.	PAGE.
Prospect Point in 1835 (Fac-simile),	W. H. Bartlett,	47
Terrapin Tower, Bridge and Falls in 1837 (Fac-simile),	W. H. Bartlett,	49
Lewiston from the Mountain,	F. C. Bromley,	50
The Fall of Table Rock,	F. C. Bromley,	53
Terrapin Rocks,	———	54
They Bore the Weary Dead back to his Desolate Cottage,	A. Mies,	57
Sister Islands and Horse-Shoe Falls,	F. C. Bromley,	58
Flower Vase and Initial,	Chas. Volkmar,	60
Steps to Rapids on Outer Sister Island,	Al. Trumble,	61
Wild Blossoms,	———	62
The Spring on Goat Island,	Chas. Volkmar,	63
American Falls from the River,	Bartlett,	64
General View of Falls in 1835,	Tom Cole,	67
Old Wind Mill at Fort Erie,	Drake,	68
The Outlet of Niagara River (Fac-simile),	W. H. Bartlett,	69
Niagara River from Original Maps,	———	70
Cynthia Island,	Chas. Volkmar,	71
Rock of Ages and Cave of the Winds,	Chas. Volkmar,	73
Farewell,	———	74
The Leaping Rock,	F. C. Bromley,	76
Shadow of the Rock and Inclined Railway,	F. C. Bromley,	77
Fort Niagara in 1814,	H. W. Troy,	79
American Rapids from Bath Island,	Chas. Volkmar,	83
Canadian Rapids above the Falls,	F. C. Bromley,	87
The Whirlpool and Manitou Rock (Fac-simile),	Bartlett,	90
Tempest,	.	91
The Maid of the Mist Going Through the Whirlpool Rapids,	E. Brown,	93
American Fall and Initial,	F. R. Green,	94
The Central Fall,	———	95
The New Suspension Bridge,	———	97
The Spirit of the Falls,	F. R. Green,	98
On Lake Ontario,	F. C. Bromley,	99
General View of Falls from Canada,	———	101
Falls View Station,	F. C. Bromley,	102
Profile of American Fall,	F. C. Bromley,	102
Along the Burning Spring Drive,	Aldine,	103
A Glimpse of American Fall,	McLean,	104
First Bridge across American Rapids to Goat Island,	G. Oakley,	105
To Lundy's Lane,	———	106
American Falls from Goat Island,	F. C. Bromley,	109
Ice Forms,	C. Maurand,	110
Behind the Horse-Shoe Falls,	F. C. Bromley,	111
Captain Webb in the Rapids,	E. Brown,	114
Matthew Webb—Portrait,	———	115

SUBJECT.	ARTIST.	PAGE
Pilgrimage under the Falls,	——	117
Below the Whirlpool,	——	119
New Cantilever Bridge,	——	121
The Bridge at Various Stages,	——	125
An Old Settler,	——	127
Section at Niagara Falls,	CHAS. LYELL,	131
Section of the Strata from Lake Ontario to Lake Erie,	HALL'S REPORT,	134
Bird's-Eye View of the Country around Niagara Falls,	J. FLEMING,	137
The Devil's Hole,	A. MIES,	139
The Cataract by Electric Light,	ALFRED TRUMBLE,	145
Horse-Shoe Falls from Ferry Road,	CHAS. VOLKMAR,	148
Leaves from a Sketch Book,	F. R. GREEN,	149
Transfer, Sir!	REDFIELD,	150
Rural Scene from the Heights,	BROWN,	151
Hotel Kaltenbach,	CURTIS,	151
A Guide,	——	152
Biddle Stairs,	F. C. BROMLEY,	153
Spiral Staircase,	F. C. BROMLEY,	155
Suspension Bridge,	——	155
Moss Island Bridge,	F. C. BROMLEY,	155
American Rapids,	BARTLETT,	155

INITIAL LETTERS FROM DRAWINGS OF BROMLEY, GREEN, VOLKMAR, AND OTHERS.

PHILOSOPHICAL REFLECTIONS.

COL. P. DONAN.

AMONG all the lands and nationalities of earth, America stands, in many respects, peerless, unrivaled and unrivalable. It is the broadest land ever given to any people, the grandest and most beautiful, the most varied in its attractions and its products, and the most unlimited in its capabilities and its future.

The more one rambles over this magnificent continent, our own half world, and the more he sees of its never-ending, ever-changing glories, sublimities and beauties, the greater must be his contempt for the average American tourist, who turns his back on scenes as transcendently grand, varied and enchanting as ever the sun, in all its wide celestial rounds, looked down upon; and rushes off to Europe, to loaf around fashionable hotels, wine-shops and haberdashers' stores, and then come back and prate, in mock-turtle French, of "la belle Paree," queenly "Madreed," the Lake of Como, Mont Blanc, Rome, Venice, Vesuvius and the Alps, and a hundred other places. If he chances to meet an intelligent European in his travels, the first question asked him exposes his folly, for it is a question about some one of the innumerable, sublime and wondrous objects in his own country that he has never deemed worth a visit. In view of the hegira that, each spring and summer, jams every out-bound steamer, there is urgent need of a constitutional amendment prohibiting any untutored American from going abroad until he has seen his own supremely lovely land.

It was Byron, who, when an American was introduced to him, began eagerly to question him about Niagara Falls, and on being told that he had never seen them, turned on his heel with an oath of unutterable disgust at the idea of a man coming from America to Europe without having seen that wonder of the world in his own country.

Nature never constructed a bigger combined idiot and cheap humbug than the American who goes into bogus raptures over the lakes and crags of Switzerland or Italy, while he has never seen or cared to see Niagara.

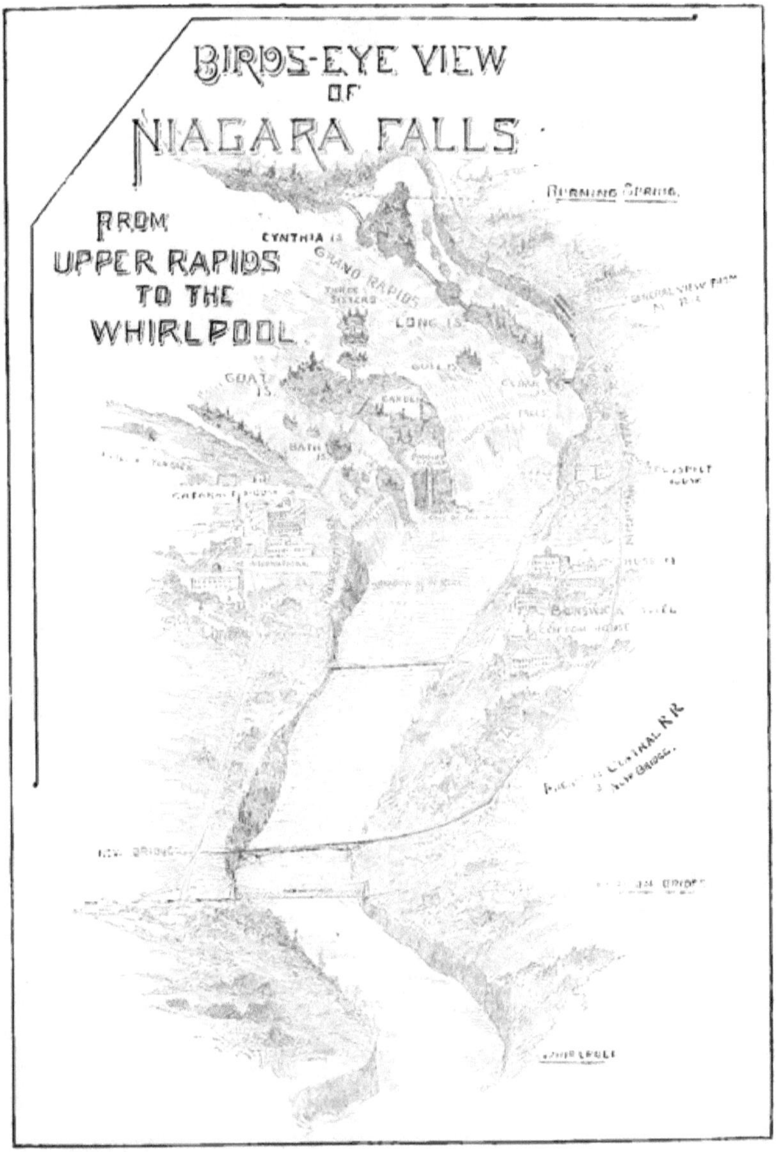
BIRDS-EYE VIEW
OF
NIAGARA FALLS
FROM
UPPER RAPIDS
TO THE
WHIRLPOOL
BURNING SPRING
CYNTHIA IS
GRAND RAPIDS
THREE SISTERS
LONG IS
GOAT IS.
BATH IS.
CENTRAL R.R.

The fall of waters! rapid as the light
The flashing mass foams shaking the abyss:
The hell of waters! where they howl and hiss,
And boil in endless torture; while the sweat
Of their great agony, wrung out from this,
Their Phlegethon, curls round the rocks of jet
That gird the gulf around, in pitiless horror set,
And mounts in spray the skies, and thence again
Returns in an unceasing shower.

EARLY GLIMPSES.

THE name NIAGARA is of Indian origin, and undoubtedly a tribal name. According to Indian authorities its orthography and pronunciation were originally ONY-A-KAR-RA, changed gradually to NI-AH-GAR-RAH. Its signification is generally given as *"Thunder of Waters."*

The work of discovery and exploration of the whole interior of the American continent is due to the zeal and enthusiasm of the French adventurers, soldiers and missionaries, of the sixteenth century. Before the Spaniards had penetrated southward, about 1539, the French, under Jacques Cartier, had sailed up the St. Lawrence as far as Quebec, in 1534.

The report of the discoveries made by Cartier's first expedition were so favorable that, under orders of King Francis I, he sailed the following year with a small flotilla, to continue investigations of the wedged-shaped river, ninety miles wide at its mouth. For many years operations did not extend beyond the site of Quebec, and information as to the source of the St. Lawrence was gathered from Indians, who told the navigator of a great lake into which also emptied a river from the south, and that upon that river and beyond the lake he would find an immense *cataract* and *portage*.

Samuel de Champlain, sent from France in 1603 for the express purpose of utilizing the discoveries made on the St. Lawrence, does not appear to have pushed his explorations on Lake Ontario in the direction of the Falls of Niagara, and leaves only an indication of the cataract on a map, published about 1613.

Creuxio, the author of a History of Canada, published in 1660, also marks it down upon his map, but makes no mention whatever in the history itself.

Other early accounts in which the cataract is incidentally mentioned are in existence, but its first description by an eye-witness did not occur until the time of La Salle's expedition to the Upper Lakes.

LA SALLE'S EXPLORATIONS.

ROBERT CAVALIER DE LA SALLE, son of a wealthy merchant of Rouen, France, an ambitious, bold, resolute young man, came to Canada in the spring of 1666, and stood conspicuous among the most adventurous explorers at that time. He had a firm belief that the Mississippi river emptied southward into the Gulf of Mexico, and not into the Pacific ocean, as stated by other discoverers, and it became the settled purpose of his life to be the instrument by which the immense territory tributary to its waters would be thrown into the lap of France, and extensive commercial relations established.

After a visit to King Louis XIV., who granted him a seigniory of land in Canada around Ft. Catarauqui, and the  order of the Knighthood, La Salle on his return rebuilt the fort, which he named Frontenac, with massive towers of stone, then took steps to place another fort at the mouth of the Niagara river, having obtained reluctant permission from the Senecas to erect it, and also to build a vessel above the falls of Niagara. This vessel, named the Griffin, launched on the 7th of August, 1679, was the first to navigate the lakes.

Father Louis Hennepin, a Roman Catholic Missionary, accompanied La Salle in his explorations. In a work he published in 1697 we find the first description of the wonderful cataract which he had visited in December, 1678. His work is entitled, "A New Discovery of a Vast Country in America, extending above four thousand miles, between New France and New Mexico, with a description of the Great Lakes, Cataracts, Rivers, Plants and Animals; also the Manners, Customs and Languages of the several Native Indians, and the Advantages of Commerce with these different Nations, etc." It contains many wonderful recitals, bearing a strong impress of Indian folk-lore and traditions, coupled with a tendency to the marvellous.

HENNEPIN'S ACCOUNT.

BETWIXT the Lakes Ontario and Erie, there is a vast and prodigious cadence of water, which falls down after a surprising and astounding manner; insomuch that the universe does not afford its parallel. 'Tis true, Italy and Suedland boast of some such things, but we may well say that they are but sorry patterns when compared to this of which we now speak. At the foot of this horrible precipice we meet with the river Niagara, which is not above a quarter of a league broad, but is wonderfully deep in some places. It is so rapid above this descent that it violently hurries down the wild beasts while endeavoring to pass it to feed on the other side, they not being able to withstand the force of its current, which inevitably casts them headlong, above six hundred feet high.

This wonderful downfall is compounded of two great cross streams of water and two falls, with an isle sloping along the middle of it. The waters which fall from this horrible precipice do foam and boil after the most hideous manner imaginable, making an outrageous noise, more terrible than that of thunder; for when the wind blows out of the south, their dismal roaring may be heard more than fifteen leagues off.

The river Niagara, having thrown itself down this incredible precipice, continues its impetuous course for two leagues together, to the Great Rock, with an inexpressible rapidity; but having passed that, its impetuosity relents, gliding along more gently for two other leagues, till it arrives at the Lake Ontario or Frontenac.

Any barque or greater vessel may pass from the fort to the top of the huge rock mentioned. This rock lies to the westward and is cut off from the land by the river Niagara, about two leagues farther down than the Great Fall, for which two leagues the people are obliged to transport their goods over land; but the way is very good, and the trees are but few, chiefly firs and oaks.

From the Great Fall unto this rock, which is to the west of the river, the two brinks of it are so prodigious high that it would make one tremble to look steadily upon the water, rolling along with a rapidity not to be imagined.

I could not conceive how it came to pass that four great lakes, the least of which is four hundred leagues in compass, should empty themselves into one another, and then all centre and discharge themselves at this Great Fall, and yet not drown a good part of America. What is yet more surprising, the ground, from the mouth of Lake Erie down to the Great Fall, appears almost level and flat. It is scarce discernible that there is the least rise or fall for six leagues together. The more than ordinary swiftness of the stream is the only thing which makes it to be observed. And that which makes it yet the stranger is that for two leagues together below the Fall, towards Lake Ontario or Frontenac, the lands are as level as they are above it, or towards Lake Erie.

Our surprise was still greater when we observed that there was no mountain within two good leagues of this cascade; and yet the vast quantity of water which is discharged by these four fresh seas, stops or centres here, and so falls above six hundred feet deep down into a gulf which one cannot look upon without horror. Two other great outlets or falls of water which are on the two sides of a small sloping island, which is in the midst, fall gently and without noise, and so glide away quietly enough; but when this prodigious quantity of water, of which I speak, comes to the fall, there is a din and noise, more deafening than the loudest thunder.

The rebounding of these waters is so great that a sort of cloud arises from the foam of it which is seen hanging over this abyss, even at noon-day, when the sun is at its height. In the midst of summer, when the weather is hottest, they rise above the tallest firs, and other great trees which grow on the sloping island which makes the two falls of water that I spoke of.

I wished an hundred times that somebody had been with us who could have described the wonders of this prodigious Fall, so as to give the reader a just and natural idea of it, such as might satisfy him, and cause in him an admiration of this prodigy of nature as great as it deserves. In the meantime accept the following draft, such as it is, in which, however, I have endeavored to give the curious reader as just an image of it as I can.

After the river has run violently for six leagues, it meets with a small sloping island, about half a quarter of a league long, and near three hundred feet broad, as well as one can guess by the eye; for it is impossible to come at it in a canoe of bark, the water runs with that force. The isle is full of cedar and fir, but the land of it lies no higher than that on the banks of the river. It seems to be all level, even as far as the two great cascades that make the main Fall.

The two sides of the channels, which are made by the isle, and run on both sides of it, overflow almost the very surface of the earth of the said isle, as well as the land that lies on the banks of the river to the east and west, as it runs south and north. But we must observe, that at the end of the isle, on the side of the two Great Falls, there is a sloping rock which reaches as far as the great gulf into which the said water falls, and yet the rock is not at all wetted by the two cascades, which fall on both sides, because the two torrents which are made by the isle throw themselves with a prodigious force, one towards the east and the other towards the west, from off the end of the isle where the Great Fall of all is.

FAC-SIMILE OF A VIEW OF NIAGARA FALLS IN FATHER LOUIS HENNEPIN

After these two torrents have thus run by the two sides of the isle, they cast their waters all of a sudden down into the gulf by two great falls; which waters are pushed so violently on by their own weight, and so sustained by the swiftness of the motion that they do not wet the rock in the least. And here it is that they tumble down into an abyss six hundred feet in depth.

The waters that flow on the side of the east do not throw themselves with that violence as those that fall on the west; the reason is, because the rock at the end of the island rises something more on this side than it does on the west; and so the waters, being supported by it somewhat longer than they are on the other side, are carried the smoother off; but on the west, the rock sloping more, the waters, for want of support, become sooner broken, and fall with greater precipitation. Another reason is, the lands that lie on the west are lower than those that lie on the east. We also observed that the waters of the fall that is to the west made a sort of square figure as they fell, which made a third cascade, less than the other two, which fell betwixt the south and north.

And because there is a rising ground which lies before these two cascades to the north, the gulf is much larger there than to the east. Moreover, we must observe that from the rising ground which lies over against the last two falls, which are on the west of the main fall, one may go down as far as the bottom of this terrible gulf. The author of this discovery was down there, the more narrowly to observe the fall of these prodigious cascades. From thence we could discover a spot of ground which lay under the fall of water which is to the east, big enough for four coaches to drive abreast without being wet; but because the ground which is to the east of the sloping rock, where the first fall empties itself into the gulf, is very steep and perpendicular, it is impossible for a man to get down on that side, into the place where the four coaches may go abreast, or to make his way through such a quantity of water as falls towards the gulf; so that it is very probable that to this dry place it is that the rattlesnakes retire, by certain passages which they find under ground.

From the end of this island it is that these two great falls of water, as also the third but now mentioned, throw themselves, after a most surprising manner, down into a dreadful gulf, six hundred feet and more in depth. I have already said that the waters which discharge themselves at the cascade to the east, fall with lesser force; whereas those at the west tumble all at once, making two cascades, one moderate, the other very violent and strong, which at last make a kind of crochet or square figure, falling from south to north and west to east. After this they rejoin the waters of the other cascade that falls to the east, and so tumble down altogether, though unequally, into the gulf, with all the violence that can be imagined from a fall of six hundred feet, which makes the most frightful cascade in the world.

I have often heard talk of the cataracts of the Nile, which make the people deaf that live near them. I know not if the Iroquois, who formerly inhabited near this fall, and lived upon wild beasts which from time to time are borne down by the violence of its torrent, withdrew themselves from its neighborhood lest they should likewise become deaf, or out of the continual fear they were in of rattlesnakes, which are very common in this place during the great heats, and lodge in the holes of the rocks as far as the mountains, which lie two leagues lower."

BARON LA HONTAINE.

WITHIN a few years after that of Father Hennepin comes the report of Baron La Hontaine, whose impressions we find recorded in a volume of "New Voyages to North America," published in London during the year 1703, and originally written in the French language.

His visit occurred in the latter part of the year 1687. On account of the bitter and relentless enmity of the Iroquois against the French he was kept in constant fear of a sudden attack. His stay was brief, and in many cases his examinations only superficial. Of the cataract, he says:

"As for the waterfall of Niagara, 'tis seven or eight hundred feet high and half a league broad. Towards the middle of it we descry an island, leaning towards the precipice as if it were ready to fall. All the beasts that do attempt to cross the waters within half a quarter of a league above this unfortunate island are sucked in by the stream. They serve for food for the Iroquois, who take them out of the water with their canoes. Between the surface of the water, that shelves off prodigiously, and the foot of the precipice, three men may cross it abreast, without any other damage than a sprinkling of some few drops of water.

THE ESTIMATE concerning the height of the Falls given by Father Hennepin and Baron La Hontaine seems greatly exaggerated. We must remember, however, that it comes from men little used to estimating distances. Even at this date, a view from the river below the Falls will produce upon most persons a much exaggerated impression. The rush of waters in front of the observer apparently comes down in a tremendous stream from the arched vaults of the heavens above.

THE FIGURES given by Charlevoix in 1721 were undoubtedly obtained with a view to an accurate estimation of the height of the Falls, and present a correct statement of the case. "For my own part, having examined it on all sides, where it could be viewed to the greatest advantage, I am inclined to think we cannot allow it less than one hundred and forty or fifty feet." (In the measure of the time, this gives the exact height to a fraction.)

GENERAL VIEW OF THE FALLS OF NIAGARA BY WELD IN 1796.
[FACSIMILE.]

EIGHTEENTH CENTURY NOTES.

PETER KALM, a noted Swedish botanist, who visited the Falls in 1750, corroborates the statement of Father Hennepin about a rock projecting upon the west side of the river which turned a part of the water at right angles with the Main Fall, thus forming a Cross Fall. He speaks of a precipitation of the rocks at a point where the water was turned originally out of its direct course, as having occurred a few years previous to his visit, and upon his plan of the Falls indicates the precise spot, which corresponds to that stated by Hennepin.

A somewhat doubtful story given in his narrative, is that of two Indians, who having been cast upon the island in the middle of the Fall (Goat Island), in order to escape made rope ladders from the bark of trees, with which they lowered themselves down to the river. Feeling unable to swim against "the waves of the eddy which, again and again, threw them with violence against the rocks, they were obliged to climb up their stairs again to the island, not knowing what to do. After some time they perceived Indians on the opposite shore, to whom they cried out. These pitied them, but gave them little hopes of help; yet they made haste down to the fort, and told the French commander where two of their brethren were. He persuaded them to try all possible means of relieving the two poor Indians; and it was done in this manner: The water that runs on the east side of the island is shallow, and breaks in rapids over the rocks. The commandant caused poles to be made and pointed with iron; two Indians determined to walk to this island by the help of these poles, to save the others or perish. They took leave of their friends, as if they were going to die. Each had two such poles in his hand, to set against the bottom of the stream to keep them steady; so they went and got to the island, and having given poles to the poor Indians there, they all returned safely to the main shore. The unfortunate creatures had been nine days on the island, and were almost starved to death."

ABBÉ PICQUET.

L' ABBÉ PICQUET, in 1751, speaks in positive terms of the number of waterfalls. He says: "This cascade is as prodigious by reason of its height and the quantity of water which falls there, as on account of the variety of its falls, which are to the number of six principal ones divided by a small island, leaving three to the north and three to the south. They produce of themselves a singular symmetry and wonderful effect."

WELD'S VISIT.

TWO SKETCHES made upon the spot by the English artist Weld in 1796, and reproduced in exact fac-simile, give the reader a most correct idea of the general appearance of the Falls at the close of the Eighteenth Century, as well as the peculiar form of the Horse-Shoe. Weld speaks in decided terms of a change in the features of the Horse-Shoe Fall, saying: "Within the memory of many of the present inhabitants of the country, the falls have receded several yards. Tradition tells us that the Great Fall instead of having been in the form of a horse shoe, once projected in the middle. For a century past, however, it has remained nearly in the present form." He also says that he saw the clouds of spray from the falls, while sailing on Lake Erie at a distance of fifty-four miles. A comparison of his sketches with that of Father Hennepin will convey at a glance the great changes of a century.

This writer is, in a measure, addicted to the marvellous, and his statements are somewhat inconsistent. The stubborn fact is, there is nothing known of the falls beyond Hennepin's day, which can be sustained either by historical or traditional record."

ARROWSMITH observes: "A person may go to the bottom of the falls, and take shelter behind the torrent, between the falling water and the precipice, where there is a space sufficient to contain a number of persons in perfect safety, and where conversation may be held without interruption from the noise."

DISTANT VIEW OF NIAGARA FALLS, 1884.

INDIAN LEGENDS

LEGENDARY associations do not abound around Niagara. The aborigines viewed the great cataract with religious veneration, as if it were a true Divinity. They displayed their adoration to the Great Spirit of the Fall by casting their pipes, wampum and different trinkets into the flood, and, it is said, the belief existed among them that the cataract demands a yearly sacrifice of two human victims. The story is charmingly and strikingly told in George Houghton's poem on Niagara. Let us abandon our prosaic effort, leaving absolute sway to the poet.

" Here, when the world was wreathed with the scarlet and gold of October,
Here, from far-scattered camps, came the moccasined tribes of the red-man.
Left in their tents their bows, forgot their brawls and dissensions,
Ringed thee with peaceful fires, and over their calumets pondered;

" Chose from their fairest virgins the fairest and purest among them,
Hollowed a birchen canoe, and fashioned a seat for the virgin,
Clothed her in white, and set her adrift to whirl to thy bosom,
Saying: 'Receive this our vow, Niagara, Father of Waters!'

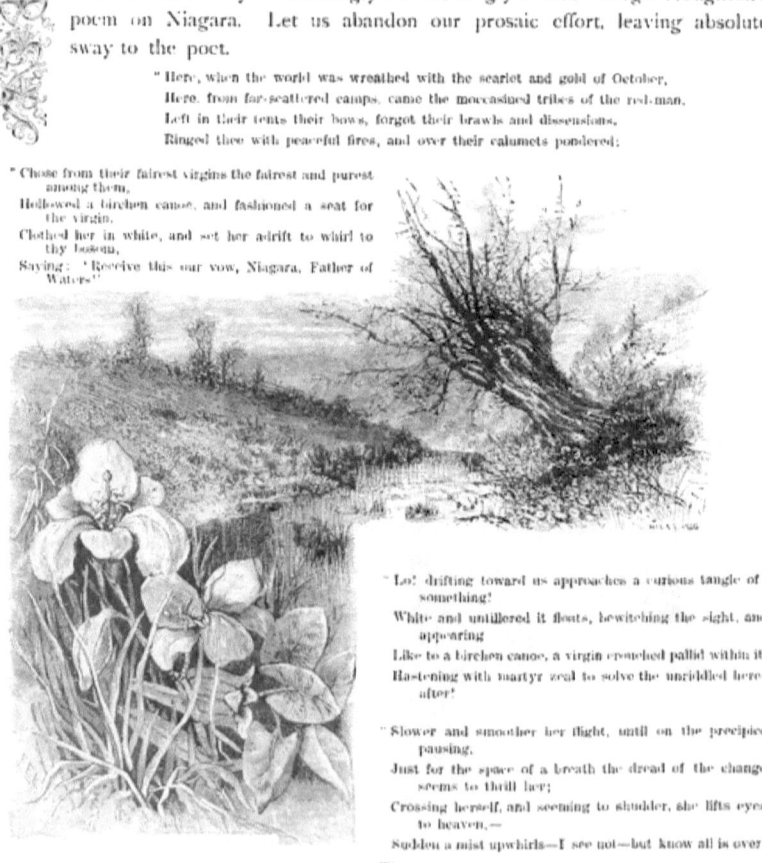

" Lo! drifting toward us approaches a curious tangle of something!
White and unlittered it floats, bewitching the sight, and appearing
Like to a birchen canoe, a virgin crouched pallid within it,
Hastening with martyr zeal to solve the unriddled hereafter!

" Slower and smoother her flight, until on the precipice pausing,
Just for the space of a breath the dread of the change seems to thrill her;
Crossing herself, and seeming to shudder, she lifts eyes to heaven,—
Sudden a mist upwhirls—I see not—but know all is over.

THE INDIAN'S LEAP — NIAGARA FALLS.

RED JACKET.

"The Last of the Senecas."

THE GREAT orator of the Senecas, the famous chief Red Jacket, whose Indian name was *Sa-go-ye-wat-ha*, or "*He keeps them awake*," has been designated as "The last of the Senecas." His eloquence was the glory of his people, and he left no one behind to fill his place at the council-fire. Opposed to the occupation of the territory of the Six Nations by the whites, his voice was ever raised upon all occasions to deprecate the cession of any lands, and so long as he lived he exerted himself to the utmost to prevent it. Yet, he lived long enough to mourn the loss, by piece-meal, of almost the entire beautiful region over which his race had held sway from the early days of tradition.

Speaking in council of the transaction between the Indians and the whites, from the first settlement of the country down to that day, he made use of this figurative illustration, addressing himself to the Commissioner who had just communicated the desire of the United States, that the Senecas should sell their lands: "We first knew you," said he, "a feeble plant which wanted a little earth whereon to grow. We gave it you,—and afterward, when we could have trod you under our feet we watered and protected you;—and now you have grown to be a mighty tree whose top reaches the clouds, and whose branches overspread the whole land; whilst we, who were then the tall pine of the forest, have become the feeble plant, and need your protection."

The name of 'Red Jacket' by which the old chief was so familiarly known to the white people, was acquired through the peculiarity of his dress. During the war of the American Independence he received from a British officer a richly embroidered scarlet jacket which he wore until it became a mark of distinction and gave him the name by which he was best known. He died on the 20th of January, 1830, in his house at the Seneca village, near Buffalo, at the probable age of eighty years. Less than nine years had elapsed after his decease when every remaining foot of the ancient inheritance of the Senecas was ceded to the white man.

PORTRAIT OF RED JACKET
FROM WEIR'S PAINTING ENGRAVED BY DANFORTH
(Facsimile.)

BELOW THE GREAT FALL.

JOHN M. DUNCAN.

DESIROUS of getting to the bottom of the Great Fall, I made my way below over scattered rocks, and surveyed the wondrous scene before me, mentally comparing the view of the falls from below with that which I had enjoyed from Table-Rock. Of the magnitude and force of the descending torrents, we have here a much more impressive conception, for as we see no part of the rapids above, and indeed nothing of the flood till it has begun its descent from the cliff, the mind is occupied almost entirely with the height and width and grandeur of the two enormous cascades. We look up in amazement at the uninterrupted pouring of so vast an accumulation of waters; and were this the only view which could be obtained, it would seem an inscrutable mystery from what source so immeasurable a volume of fresh water could be constantly poured forth.

The noise of the falls is of course greatly increased below; indeed it thunders in the ear most overpoweringly. I use the term *thunders* for want of a more appropriate one, but it by no means conveys any adequate idea of the awfully deep and unvarying sound.

To heighten the splendor of the scene, a magnificent rainbow, pencilled on the clouds of spray, and perfectly unbroken from end to end, overarched the space between the one bank and the other, at the widest part. This in so entire a state is rather a rare occurrence, for though the prismatic colors are always visible during sunshine, floating in little fragments here and there, they only unite into a regular bow in particular positions of the sun, and never complete the semi-circular curve but when the air, as happened on this occasion, is perfectly calm.

A beautiful moonlight evening succeeded, and so favorable an opportunity of another view was not to be neglected. The moon's rays fell directly upon the American cascade, leaving the greater part of the other fall in deep shadow. The spray appeared to rise in greatly increased volumes, and the dim light mingling with its haze, and accompanied by a perceptible increase in the sound of the cataracts, imparted to the whole a peculiar sublimity which was wanting in daylight.

HORSE-SHOE FALLS FROM BELOW.

CREATION'S PRIDE.

Niagara's cañon, swept by waters grand!
  No gorge like thine, nor depths, the mighty hand
    Of time hath wrought.

Thy cataract stupendous is, and fierce;
  No human voice or sound can ever pierce
    Its deaf'ning roar.

Thy seething currents rend with awful might
  Great rocks, that nature in chaotic night
    Didst rear on high.

A whirlpool deep within thy walls doth hiss,
  And, raging 'round, sinks down in dark abyss
    To unknown depths.

Around Ontario's blue and wide domain,
  No mountains check, nor lofty barriers chain,
    Thine outlet vast.

In the great ocean's infinite expanse
  Thy volumes rest, and with their powers, enhance
    The vasty deep.
            — Wilhelm Mentzer.

THE OLD FERRY LANDING.

QUAINT and curious was the Landing of the ferry on the American side fifty years ago. In those days people took whole weeks to view the falls, and delighted in ascending leisurely the rugged stairs and path, stopping and turning round almost at each step to drink in the ever-changing glories of the scene.

"The cliff and staircase at this Landing," says Willis, "would be considered highly picturesque anywhere but at the side of Niagara. The hundred stairs clinging to the rock, the wild vines overgrowing the temporary shed under which

travellers take shelter from the spray, the descending and ascending figures, and the athletic boatmen, whose occupation of pulling across this troubled ferry requires herculean strength and proportions, all form a subject for the painter, which could only be disregarded amid the engrossing scenes of Niagara."

When the mania to improve Nature's own work seized the property owners around the falls, the old landing and staircase had to disappear and make way for quicker means of transit. This picturesque old landmark is gone, and in its place stands the unartistic and unpicturesque but nevertheless convenient inclined railway.

AMERICAN RAPIDS.

N. P. WILLIS.

THE RAPIDS are far from being the least interesting feature of Niagara. There is a violence and a power in their foaming career, which is seen in no phenomenon of the same class. Standing on the bridge which connects Goat Island with the Main, and looking up towards Lake Erie, the leaping crests of the rapids form the horizon, and it seems like a battle-charge of tempestuous waves, animated and infuriated against the sky.

No one who has not seen this spectacle of turbulent grandeur can conceive with what force the swift and overwhelming waters are flung upwards. The rocks, whose soaring points show above the surface, seem tormented with some supernatural agony, and fling off the wild and hurried waters, as if with the force of a giant's arm. Nearer the plunge of the Fall, the Rapids become still more agitated; and it is almost impossible for the spectator to rid himself of the idea, that they are conscious of the abyss to which they are hurrying, and struggle back in the very extremity of horror.

This propensity to invest Niagara with a soul and human feelings is a common effect upon the minds of visitors, in every part of its wonderful phenomena. The torture of the Rapids, the clinging curves with which they embrace the small rocky islands that live amid the surge, the sudden calmness at the brow of the cataract, and the infernal writhe and whiteness with which they reappear, powerless from the depths of the abyss, all seem, to the excited imagination of the gazer, like the natural effects of impending ruin, desperate resolution, and fearful agony, on the minds and frames of mortals.

During the Canadian war of 1814, General Putnam, the famous partisan soldier, made the first descent upon Goat Island. A wager had been laid, that no man in the army would dare to cross the Rapids from the American side; and with the personal daring for which he was remarkable, above all the men of that trying period, he undertook the feat. Selecting the four stoutest and most resolute men in his corps, he embarked in a batteau just above the island, and with a rope attached to the ring-bolt, which was held by as many muscular fellows on the shore, he succeeded by desperate rowing in reaching his mark. He most easily towed back, and the feat has since been rendered unnecessary by the construction of the bridge from the main land to Goat Island.

NIAGARA.

"Tremendous torrent! for an instant hush
The terrors of thy voice, and cast aside
Those wide involving shadows, that my eyes
May see the fearful beauty of thy face!
* * * * *
Thou flowest on in quiet, till thy waves
Grow broken 'midst the rocks; thy current then
Shoots onward like the irresistible course
Of destiny. Ah, terribly they rage,—
The hoarse and rapid whirlpools there! My brain
Grows wild, my senses wander, as I gaze
Upon the hurrying waters; and my sight
Vainly would follow, as toward the verge
Sweeps the wide torrent. Waves innumerable
Meet there and madden,— waves innumerable
Urge on and overtake the waves before,
And disappear in thunder and in foam.

They reach, they leap the barrier,— the abyss
Swallows insatiable the sinking waves.
A thousand rainbows arch them, and woods
Are deafened with the roar. The violent shock
Shatters to vapor the descending sheets.
A cloudy whirlwind fills the gulf, and heaves
The mighty pyramid of circling mist
To heaven. * * * *
What seeks my restless eye? Why are not here,
About the jaws of this abyss, the palms,—
Ah, the delicious palms,— that on the plains
Of my own native Cuba spring and spread
Their thickly foliaged summits to the sun,
And, in the breathings of the ocean air
Wave soft beneath the heaven's unspotted blue?

But no, Niagara,— thy forest pines
Are fitter coronal for thee. The palm,
The effeminate myrtle and pale rose may grow
In gardens and give out their fragrance there,
Unmanning him who breathes it. Thine it is
To do a nobler office. Generous minds
Behold thee, and are moved and learn to rise
Above earth's frivolous pleasures; they partake
Thy grandeur at the utterance of thy name.
* * * * *
Dread torrent, that with wonder and with fear
Dost overwhelm the soul of him who looks
Upon thee, and dost bear it from itself,—
Whence hast thou thy beginning? Who supplies
Age after age, thy unexhausted springs?
What power hath ordered that, when all thy weight
Descends into the deep, the swollen waves
Rise not and roll to overwhelm the earth?

The Lord hath opened his omnipotent hand,
Covered thy face with clouds and given his voice
To thy down-rushing waters; he hath girt
Thy terrible forehead with his radiant bow.
I see thy never-resting waters run,
And I bethink me how the tide of time
Sweeps to eternity."

*Translated from the Spanish of Maria Jos' Heredonia,
by William Cullen Bryant.*

"THY FOREST PINES ARE FITTEST CORONAL."

ALBUM SKETCH.

BY COL. PORTER.

AN ARTIST, underneath his sign (a masterpiece, of course)
Had written, to prevent mistakes, 'This represents a horse';
So ere I send my Album Sketch, less connoisseurs should err,
I think it well my Pen should be my Art's interpreter.

"A chieftain of the Iroquois, clad in a bison's skin,
Had led two travelers through the wood, La Salle and Hennepin.
He points, and there they, standing, gaze upon the ceaseless flow
Of waters falling as they fell two hundred years ago.

"Those three are gone, and little heed our worldly gain or loss
The Chief, the Soldier of the Sword, the Soldier of the Cross.
One died in battle, one in bed, and one by secret foe;
But the waters fall as once they fell two hundred years ago.

"Ah, me! what myriads of men, since then, have come and gone;
What states have risen and decayed, what prizes lost and won;
What varied tricks the juggler, Time, has played with all below.
But the waters fall as once they fell two hundred years ago.

"What troops of tourists have encamped upon the river's brink;
What poets shed from countless quills Niagaras of ink;
What artist armies tried to fix the evanescent bow
Of the waters falling as they fell two hundred years ago.

    *   *   *   *   *   *   *   *   *

"And stately inns feed scores of guests from well replenished larder,
And hackmen drive their horses hard, but drive a bargain harder;
And screaming locomotives rush in anger to and fro;
But the waters fall as once they fell two hundred years ago.

"And brides of every age and clime frequent the island's bower,
And gaze from off the stone-built perch—hence called the Bridal Tower—
And many a lunar belle goes forth to meet a lunar beau,
By the waters falling as they fell two hundred years ago.

"And bridges bind thy breast, O stream! and buzzing mill-wheels turn,
To show, like Samson, thou art forced thy daily bread to earn;
And steamers splash thy milk-white waves, exulting as they go.
But the waters fall as once they fell two hundred years ago.

"Thy banks no longer are the same that early travelers found them,
But break and crumble now and then like other banks around them;
And on their verge our life sweeps on—alternate joy and woe;
But the waters fall as once they fell two hundred years ago.

"Thus phantoms of a by-gone age have melted like the spray,
And in our turn we too shall pass, the phantoms of to-day;
But the armies of the coming time shall watch the ceaseless flow
Of waters falling as they fell two hundred years ago."

"THE CHIEF, THE SOLDIER OF THE SWORD, THE SOLDIER OF THE CROSS."

BEHIND THE SHEET OF WATER.

CHAS. A. MURRAY.

ET HIM whose spirit delights in the awful sublimity of nature, who loves the war of elements, and the secret and mysterious paths of darkness, descend from the Table-Rock, and undeterred by the wind and spray that will appear to oppose his entrance,—let him walk along a narrow ledge that extends about one hundred feet under the great Horse-Shoe Fall, and there, with his back to the huge beetling rock, above him the canopy of rushing waters, before him and all around a tempestuous whirlwind of foam, and beneath his feet a raging and boiling unfathomed abyss,—let him meditate on the littleness of man, and on the attributes of Him who metes out those waters in the hollow of his hand.

When I followed the guide into this stormy recess, there was a strong breeze of wind, and the spray was dashed against our faces with such unusual violence as to render it almost impossible upon first entering, to keep the eyes open, or to respire. However, by slouching the hat over my eyes and holding my breath, I followed the guide without difficulty to the interior of the rocky chambers where the spray and whirlwind are less violent, and where the faculties of seeing, hearing and feeling are restored. I pursued the little path or ledge to its farthest extremity, at a point called Termination Rock; and, seating myself, regardless of the "pelting of the pitiless storm," I revelled in the glorious and terrible scene before me. To describe it further I will not attempt.

CAPTAIN HALL'S NARRATIVE.

ON FIRST coming to a scene so stupendous and varied as that of Niagara, the attention is embarrassed by the crowd of new objects; and it always requires a certain degree of time to arrange the images which are suggested, before they can be duly appreciated. After reaching the Falls, we had still enough of daylight to take a hasty view of them before going to bed; and whether it was owing to the jolting of the rough roads, or to the fatigue of over-excited admiration, I do not know, but I soon dropped into a profound sleep, in spite of all the roaring close at hand. About two o'clock in the morning, while I was dreaming of one particular part of the fall, called the Horse-Shoe, which had struck me as being more particularly solemn than all the rest put together, I was awakened by a feeble cry from my little girl, and set off in quest of a light. In groping along the passages, I came accidentally to an open window, where my ear was arrested by the loud splashing noise of the rapids above the falls, dashing past, immediately under the veranda. The deep sound of the more distant cascade was also heard, far louder, and quite different in kind from that of the rapids. For the first time I became conscious of the full magnificence of the scene.

The night was very dark, though the stars were out, twinkling and flashing over the cataract; and there rose a damp, earthy smell from the ground, as if the dew had been settling heavily upon it; or perhaps it might be the spray from the falls. There was not the slightest breath of wind to shake the drops from the leaves, and I stood for some time endeavoring to recollect what I had met with before that resembled this. The hollow sound of the surf at Madras was at length brought to my thoughts as the nearest thing to it.

ON GOAT ISLAND.

The Falls are divided into two parts by Goat Island, on which we passed the greater part of the next day. We walked round the Island several times in the course of the day, and though it affords a great variety of admirable views of the falls, and also of the rapids, both on the American and on the English sides of the river, we always found ourselves drawn back irresistibly to the Great Horse-Shoe, where the largest portion of the stream passes on a concave edge, and where, from its depth, I suppose, it acquires a deep green color, seen at no other part of the cascade; almost all the rest being nearly snow-white.

In hunting for similes to describe what we saw and heard, we were quite agreed that the sound of the falls most nearly resembles that of a grist mill, of large dimensions. There is precisely the same incessant, rumbling, deep, monotonous sound, accompanied by the tremor, which is observable in a building where many pairs of millstones are at work. This tremulous effect extends to the distance of several hundred yards from the river; but is most conspicuous on Goat Island, which stands in the center between the two falls. The noise of the rapids is also loud, but much sharper, and varies a good deal with the situation of the listener. We were walking one day along a path in the woods on the island, at  some distance from the Great Cataract, and there, it struck me, the sound of the rapids resembled not a little the noise caused by a heavy shower of rain on the leaves of a forest in a calm.

The scenery in the neighborhood of Niagara has, in itself, little or no interest, and has been rendered still less attractive by the erection of hotels, paper manufactories, saw-mills, and numerous other raw, staring, wooden edifices. Perhaps it is quite as well that it should be so; because any scenery which should be in keeping with the grand object which gives its character to this wonderful spot, would, in all probability, diminish the effect produced by its standing on its own merits.

THE FIRST GOAT ISLAND BRIDGE.

It has been said that there is always something about a bridge which interests, more or less. If it be not picturesque in itself, it may be curious in its structure, or high, or long, or may possess something or other to attract notice. At all

VIEW OF NIAGARA FALLS FROM PROSPECT POINT
(ABRAHAM 1894)

events, the bridge which connects the main American shore with Goat Island is one of the most singular pieces of engineering in the world, and shows, not only much ingenuity, but boldness of thought in its projector, the owner of the island. It is between six and seven hundred feet in length, and is thrown across one of the worst parts of the rapids, not more than fifty yards above the crest of the American Fall. It is made of wood, and consists of seven straight portions, resting on wooden piers, so contrived as to have perfect stability, although the foundation on which they rest is extremely unequal. The bed of the river at that place is covered with rounded and angular rocks of irregular sizes. Along this rugged and steep bottom the river dashes in a torrent, covered with breakers and foam, at the rate of six or seven miles an hour, making a noise not unlike that of the sea on a shallow ledge of rocks. On the evening of the same day we drove towards Lake Ontario for six or seven miles on the right bank of the Niagara, and then crossed over to the Canada shore at Queenstown. Close to the spot where we landed there stands a monument to the gallant General Brock, who was killed during the battle of Queenstown, in the act of repelling an invasion of the frontier by the Americans during the war of 1812. The view from the top of the monument extended far over Lake Ontario, and showed us the windings of the Niagara through the low and wooded country which hangs like a rich green fringe along the southern skirt of that great sheet of water. By the time we reached the inn, close to the falls on the English side, we had barely light enough left to see the cataract from the balcony of our bedroom—distant from it, in a straight line, not a couple of hundred yards. I cannot bring myself to attempt any description of the pleasure which we experienced, while thus sitting at ease, and conscious of viewing, in sober reality, and at leisure, an object with which we had been familiar, in fancy at least, all our lives. The Falls of Niagara infinitely exceeded our anticipations, and fulfilled our expectations.

IMPRESSIONS.

JAMES STUART.

THE FIRST sight only increased our desire to have the whole scene unfolded. We hurried to the Table-Rock, which projects and looks over the falls, and to the other stations on the Canada side of the river. We afterward crossed the river in a small boat, about 200 or 300 yards below the falls, saw them from the American side, and from Goat Island, and hardly quitted the spot while daylight remained. The overwhelming sensations, with which a spectator can hardly fail to be affected, are produced by the immense flood,—not less than 100 millions of tons of water per hour,—the stupendous mass, and overpowering force of the roaring and falling waters. It is in truth a great deep ocean, thrown over a precipice 160 feet high. Every thing, every surrounding object, is viewed with indifference, while the mind is wholly absorbed in the contemplation of a spectacle so  sublime,—surpassing in majesty, and grandeur, and power, all the works of nature which have ever arrested the attention, or presented themselves to the imagination. No just or adequate description can be conveyed by language. Such words as grandeur, majesty, sublimity, fail altogether to express the feelings which so magnificent a sight, exceeding so immeasurably all of the same kind that we have ever seen or imagined, excites. Truly, as the poet says, the eye of man must see this miracle to comprehend it, or the feelings it produces.

The great volume of water, of course, inclines very much forward in its descent, projecting about fifty feet from the base, and falls, for the most part of the perpendicular height, in an unbroken sheet of dark green color, until it meets a cloud of spray ascending from the rocks below, in which it is lost to the eye.

THE HORSE-SHOE FALL.

N. P. WILLIS

THE HORSE-SHOE FALL, as a single object, is unquestionably the sublimest thing in nature. To know that the angle of the cataract, from the British shore to the tower, is near half a mile in length; that it falls so many feet with so many tons of water a minute; or even to see it, as here, admirably represented by the pencil; conveys no idea to the reader of the impression produced on the spectator. One of the most remarkable things about Niagara is entirely lost in the drawing— its *motion*. The visitor to Niagara should devote one day exclusively to the observation of this astonishing feature.

The broad flood glides out of Lake Erie with a confiding tranquility that seems to you, when you know its impending destiny, like that of a human creature advancing irresistibly, but unconsciously, to his death. He embraces the bright islands that part his arms for a caress; takes into his bosom the calm tribute of the Tonewanta and Unnekuqua—small streams that come drowsing through the wilderness—and flows on, till he has left Lake Erie far behind, bathing the curving sides of his green shores with a surface which only the summer wind ruffles. The channel begins to descend; the still unsuspecting waters fall back into curling eddies along the banks, but the current in the centre flows smoothly still. Suddenly the powerful stream is flung with accumulated swiftness among broken rocks; and, as you watch it from below, it seems tossed with the first shock into the very sky. It descends in foam, and from this moment its agony commences.

For three miles it tosses and resists, and, racked at every step by sharper rocks and increased rapidity, its unwilling and choked waves fly back, to be again precipitated onward, and at last reach the glossy curve convulsed with supernatural horror. They touch the emerald arch, and in that instant, like the calm that follows the conviction of inevitable doom, the agitation ceases,— the waters pause,— the foam and resistance subside into a transparent stillness,—and—slowly and solemnly the vexed and tormented sufferer drops into the abyss.

Every spectator, every child, is struck with the singular deliberation, the unnatural slowness, with which the waters of Niagara take their plunge. The laws of gravitation seem suspended, and the sublimity of the tremendous gulf below seems to check the descending victim on the verge, as if it paused in awe.—*American Scenery*.

VIEW OF OLD TOWER, TERRAPIN BRIDGE AND HORSESHOE FALLS IN 1837.
(Bartlett.)

A THRILLING ESCAPE.

WM. HOSEA BALLOU.

A PARTY of four, including the writer, made a survey of the interior of the canyon from Lewiston to the Suspension Bridge. The perils of such a passage are known to but few, and can only be realized by the daring adventurer who may undertake it for himself. Indeed, the foot of man scarcely ever treads this infernal region, where on every hand one is beset by untold difficulties. With great caution we clambered along, making a fearful yet intensely exciting exploration. At times the river would rise suddenly some ten or fifteen feet, as if some dam above had broken, causing a hasty retreat up the canyon's sides. From points above loose fragments of rocks precipitated themselves, causing a lively scattering beneath. An occasional rattlesnake leaped from his den in astonishment at such intrusion, only to yield his life as a penalty. Here and there gigantic bowlders reared their heads from the water's edge, necessitating a difficult and dangerous passage around or over. Once the writer saw a bird's nest on the extremity of an alder, which leaned well over the seething, whirling waters. Our approach caused a rare sparrow to flit away in alarm. Without thought, save of the acquisition of a rare egg, I threw by my coat and sprang into the branches. I had gone but half way out on the limb when a wild cry of alarm caused me to look around, just in time to see the roots of the little tree being wrenched from their place by my weight and the fierce current. I gave a spring and landed safely, just in the instant as the tree fell into the waters and was hurried out of sight. Getting into the canyon at Lewiston was comparatively easy, but making one's way out near the Falls was another thing. Nearly a mile below Devaux College, situated a little north of the railway bridge, the possibility of making our way along the river's edge ceased. Night was approaching, and a day's hard work would be required to reach Lewiston, at the foot of the canyon, from which point we entered. Above, the rocks towered several hundred feet. We had the alternative of remaining in the gorge over night, where life was momentarily uncertain, or of fighting our way over an almost impassable passage to the foot of the steps leading down from the college. We determined to accept the latter. After an hour's climb over tangled masses of fallen trees, logs, and bowlders, we made our way to a narrow ridge, one hundred feet from the top, formed of fallen *débris*. The scene from this point beggared description. Beneath was one frightful mass of rocks and trees. One false step and the fated individual would have plunged to a horrible doom. We followed the ridge for perhaps a half mile, when it came to an abrupt termination. In front were bare walls of perpendicular rocks, extending from the top one hundred feet above, straight down to the rushing waters two hundred feet below. The interim to be crossed, if possible, was several rods in breadth. Despair stalked abroad on every side. The setting sun cast his flickering rays upon an almost certain doom to the daring mortal who should attempt that passage. Just above our heads a crevice in the rocks was discovered which seemed to cross the face of the rocks. The thought of passing it was startling, but hurriedly agreed upon. There seemed to be room for the toes to cling, but the chances of a place for the hands seemed slender and treacherous.

The various instruments were divided among the party by lot, the box containing the heavy theodolite falling to the writer. The tallest clambered on to the crevice first, the others assisting and following, until the writer, smallest and last, was safely drawn up. A perilous and cautious passage began. The face of the rock was slippery, and the niches where the hand could cling few and far between. One carrying a coat on his arm, in a moment of trepidation let the garment fall, and in an instant it was whirled out of sight by the seething waters below. Another unloosed a bowlder, which took a frightful plunge downward, leaving a great open space beneath. By mutual assistance all had safely passed across, when the writer, with the heavy instrument upon his back, was midway on the passage. Here a sharp point of rock, just breast high, impeded the way. In attempting to get around this, the foot failed to find a resting place. To get under was impossible—above there was no fingerhold. The heavy instrument behind seemed to weigh down like a mountain, and was rapidly displacing the point of balance. The slender hold was relaxing; 100 feet above was the calm, safe world—250 below, the merciless waters. One foot slipped off, and was going down—down; a mist came over the eyes and all seemed lost, when the foot caught on a slender bush, a hand grasped the back and drew me on to a firm footing. Just then the sun sank from sight, but not until he saw the adventurers safe on the steps of the college.

TABLE ROCK.

AROUND Table Rock cluster some of the pleasantest and most impressive memories of the Great Falls. A projecting table-like ledge of rock, situate at the angle formed by the Horse-Shoe Fall with the Canadian bank, and in the same plane with the crest of the cataract, it has always been a favorite resort for those whose spirit delights in close and deep communion with this marvel of Nature. "He who admires Nature in her stern and magnificent array, should stand upon the Table Rock," says Murray. "There *Presentiorem Conspiciet Deum*,'—there the tremendous roar will stun his ear—the mingled masses of waters and of foam will bewilder his eye—his mind will be overwhelmed by contending feelings of elevation and depression—and, unless he be colder than the very rock on which he stands, the thoughts that press upon his brain, will be high, pure, and enthusiastic, and his hot brow will welcome the cool, light spray that is ever falling around that holy spot."

Originally an immense table of rock extending far beyond and at right angles with the waters of the Horse-Shoe; its form and dimensions have been materially changed by frequent and violent disruptions. In 1818 a mass broke off in its immediate proximity, one hundred and sixty feet in length by thirty to forty feet in width. In the latter part of 1828 and beginning of 1829, the fall of several masses occurred, leaving the table-shaped ledge without support on the north and south sides. At mid-day on the 26th of June, 1850, a terrible noise, which shook the earth, startled the inhabitants for miles around the Falls. Table Rock remained only as a memory of the past—a narrow bench along the bank. The huge mass which fell was over two hundred feet long, sixty feet wide, and one hundred feet deep where it separated from the bank. A solitary stableman, washing an omnibus on the rock, escaped with his life, the vehicle, of which no subsequent traces could be seen or found, falling into the abyss.

The general view is more extensive and effective at this point than any others, embracing, in addition to the Falls, the Canadian Rapids above, with sharp, white-crested waves, coming in rush and tumble to the calm edge of the Fall to be engulfed in an instant amid the foaming waters in the chasm below. "The ocean stretching beyond reach of vision, or swooping the sternest lee-shore, is a feebler emblem of power than is the inevitable and despairing rush with which these tortured waters plunge down. The Rapids are a fit portal for Niagara."

The sight of the gulf below is one that can never be forgotten. The water breaks into spray at the very top, and sends up a steam from the inexplorable abyss, which shrouds all below in most terrific obscurity. A portion of the vapor rises between the descending water and the rock, and comes whirling out in the most violent agitation; and the deep hollow sound of the Cataract, reverberating from the rocky caverns, completes the elements of sublimity with which the scene is charged.

Below the bank lies a rugged path leading to "Termination Rock," under the western end of the Horse-Shoe. It is reached by means of an ingeniously constructed spiral staircase, securely fastened to the rocky bank. Of the view around the base of the stairs, a writer in *Harpers' Magazine* said: "You find yourself below the overhanging mass of Table Rock. You are close at the edge of the falling water, which descends in a mass apparently as solid as though carved from marble. You now begin to comprehend the height of the Fall. It makes you dizzy to look up to the upper edge of the rushing column —you stand just midway between the top and the bottom. Above you hangs the imminent mass of Table Rock; below, far down by the wet and jagged rocks, is a boiling whirlpool, where the water writhes and eddies as though frenzied with its fearful leap. Round and round it goes in solemn gyrations, bearing with it whatever floating object may have been plunged into its vortex."

The view of the Falls from this point is unsurpassed, as it presents a scene of Niagara to the view at one instant of time, completely filling the field of vision, and giving the full impress of its grandeur and beauty to the mind. The impressiveness of the scene behind the immense sheet of the principal Cataract, will fully repay for the peril and discomfort attending upon a visit to it. The pendant roof of rock above, the arching waters, and the abyss of foam below, are objects that awaken emotions the sublimity of which is sometimes oppressive, and yet always pleasingly awful.

TERRAPIN ROCKS.

THE HERMIT OF THE FALLS.

MRS. SIGOURNEY.

DURING the year 1829, in the glow of early summer, a young stranger, of pleasing countenance and person, made his appearance at Niagara. It was at first conjectured that he might be an artist, as a large portfolio, with books and musical instruments, were observed among his baggage. He was deeply impressed by the majesty and sublimity of the Cataract, and its surrounding scenery, and expressed an intention to remain a week, that he might examine it accurately. But the fascination which all minds of sensibility feel, in the presence of that glorious work of the Creator, grew strongly upon him, and he was heard to say, that six weeks were inadequate to become acquainted with its outlines. At the end of that period he was still unable to tear himself away, and desired to build there a tabernacle, that he might indulge both in his love of solitary musings and of nature's sublimity. He applied for a spot upon the island of the Three Sisters, where he might construct a cottage after his own model, which comprised, among other peculiarities, isolation by means of a draw-bridge. Circumstances forbidding a compliance with his request, he took up his residence in an old house upon this island, which he rendered as comfortable as the state of the case would admit. Here he continued about twenty months, until the intrusion of a family interrupted his recluse habits. He then quietly withdrew, and reared for himself a less commodious shelter, near Prospect Point. His simple and favorite fare of bread and milk was readily purchased, and whenever he required other food, he preferred to prepare it with his own hands.

When bleak winter came, a cheerful fire of wood blazed upon his hearth, and by his evening lamp he beguiled the hours with the perusal of books in various languages, and with sweet music. It was almost surprising to hear, in such depth of solitude, the long drawn, thrilling tones of the viol, or the softest melodies of the flute, gushing forth from that low-browed hut, or the guitar, breathing out so lightly, amid the rush and thunder of the never-slumbering tide.

Yet, though the world of letters was familiar to his mind, and the living world to his observation, for he had travelled widely, both in his native Europe and the East, he sought not association with mankind, to unfold or to increase his stores of knowledge. Those who had heard him converse, spoke with surprise and admiration of his colloquial powers, his command of language, and the spirit of eloquence that flowed from his lips. But he seldom and sparingly admitted this intercourse, studiously avoiding society, though there seemed in his nature nothing of moroseness or misanthropy. On the contrary, he showed kindness even to the humblest animal. Birds' instinctively learned it, and freely entered his dwelling to receive from his hands crumbs or seeds.

But the absorbing delight of his existence, was communion with the mighty Niagara. Here, at every hour of the day or night, he might be seen a fervent worshipper. At gray dawn he went to visit it in its fleecy veil; at high noon, he banqueted on the full splendor of its glory; beneath the soft tinting of the lunar bow he lingered, looking for the angel's wing whose pencil had painted it; at solemn midnight, he knelt, soul-subdued, as on the foot-stool of Jehovah. Neither storms, nor the piercing cold of winter, prevented his visits to this great temple of his adoration.

When the frozen mists, gathering upon the lofty trees, seemed to have transmuted them to columns of alabaster; when every branch and shrub, and spray, glittering with transparent ice, waved in the sunbeam its coronet of diamonds, he gazed, unconscious of the keen atmosphere, charmed and chained by the rainbow-cinctured Cataract. His feet had worn a beaten path from his cottage thither. There was, at that time an extension of the Terrapin Bridge by a single shaft of timber, carried out ten feet over the fathomless abyss, where it hung tremulously, guarded only by a rude parapet.

To this point he often passed and repassed, amid the darkness of the night. He even took pleasure in grasping it with his hands, and thus suspending himself over the awful gulf; so much had his morbid enthusiasm learned to feel, and even to revel, amid the terribly sublime.

Among his favorite, daily gratifications was that of bathing. The few who interested themselves in his welfare, supposed that he pursued it to excess, and protracted it after the severity of the weather rendered it hazardous to health.

He scooped out, and arranged for himself, a secluded and romantic bath, between Moss and Iris islands. Afterwards, he formed the habit of bathing below the principal Fall. One bright, but rather chilly day, in the month of June, 1831, a man employed about the Ferry, saw him go into the water, and a long time after, observed his clothes to be still lying upon the bank.

Inquiry was made. The anxiety was but too well founded. The poor hermit had indeed taken his last bath. It was supposed that cramp might have been induced by the unwonted chill of the atmosphere or water. Still the body was not found, the depth and force of the current just below being exceedingly great. In the course of their search, they passed onward to the Whirlpool. There, amid

"THEY BORE THE WEARY DEAD BACK TO HIS DESOLATE COTTAGE."

those boiling eddies, was the pallid corpse, making fearful and rapid gyrations upon the face of the black waters. At some point of suction, it suddenly plunged and disappeared. Again emerging, it was fearful to see it leap half its length above the flood, and with a face so deadly pale, play among the tossing billows, then float motionless, as if exhausted, and anon returning to the encounter, spring, struggle, and contend like a maniac battling with mortal foes.

It was strangely painful to think that he was not permitted to find a grave even beneath the waters he had loved; that all the gentleness and charity of his nature, should be changed by death to the fury of a madman; and that the king of terrors who brings repose to the despot, and the man of blood, should teach warfare

Goat Islands And horseshoe fall from Canada

to him who had ever worn the meekness of the lamb. For days and nights this terrible purgatory was prolonged. It was on the twenty-first of June, that, after many efforts, they were enabled to bear the weary dead back to his desolate cottage.

There they found his faithful dog guarding the door. Heavily the long period had worn away, while he watched for his only friend and wondered why he delayed his coming. He scrutinized the approaching group suspiciously, and would not willingly have given them admittance, save that a low, stifled wail at length announced his intuitive knowledge of the master, whom the work of death had effectually disguised from the eyes of men.

They laid him on his bed, the thick, dripping masses of his beautiful hair clinging to and veiling the features so late expressive and comely. On the pillow was his pet kitten; to her, also, the watch for the master had been long and wearisome.

In his chair lay the guitar, whose melody was probably the last that his ear had heard on earth. There were also his flute and violin, his portfolio and books, scattered and open, as if recently used. On the spread table was the untasted meal for noon, which he had prepared against his return from that bath which had proved so fatal. It was a touching sight; the dead hermit mourned by his humble retainers, the poor animals who loved him, and ready to be laid by stranger-hands in a foreign grave.

So fell this singular and accomplished being, at the early age of twenty-eight. Learned in the languages, in the arts and sciences, improved by extensive travel, gifted with personal beauty, and a feeling heart, the motives for this estrangement from his kind are still enveloped in mystery. It was, however, known that he was a native of England, where his father was a clergyman; that he received from thence ample remittances for his comfort; and that his name was Francis Abbot. These facts had been previously ascertained, but no written papers were found in his cell, to throw additional light upon the obscurity in which he had so effectually wrapped the history of his pilgrimage.

That he was neither an ascetic nor a misanthrope, has been sufficiently proved. Why he should choose to withdraw from society, which he was so well fitted to benefit and adorn, must ever remain unexplained. That no crime had driven him thence, his blameless and pious life bore witness to all who knew him.

It might seem that no plan of seclusion had been deliberately formed, until enthusiastic admiration of the unparalleled scenery among which he was cast, induced and for two years had given it permanence. And if any one could be justified for withdrawing from life's active duties, to dwell awhile with solitude and contemplation, would it not be in a spot like this, where Nature ever speaks audibly of her majestic and glorious Author?

We visited, in the summer of 1844, the deserted abode of the hermit. It was partially ruinous, but we traced out its different compartments, and the hearth-stone where his winter evenings passed amid books and music, his faithful dog at his feet, and on his knee his playful, happy kitten.

At our entrance, a pair of nesting birds flew forth affrighted. Methought they were fitting representatives of that gentle spirit, which would not have disturbed their tenantry, or harmed the trusting sparrow.

We think with tenderness of thee, erring and lonely brother. For at the last day, when the secrets of all are unveiled, it will be found that there are sadder mistakes to deplore than thine; — time wasted idly, but not innocently — and talents perverted without the palliation of a virtuous life, the love of Nature, or the fear of God.

THE RAMBLER.

CHAS. J. B. LATROBE.

YOU MAY recollect my juvenile weakness, that of being a notorious cascade-hunter. So you may well ask what impression was made upon me by Niagara. At the commencement of the present century, Niagara, difficult of access, and rarely visited, was still the cataract of the wilderness. The red Indian still lingered in its vicinity, adored the Great Spirit and "Master of Life" as he listened to the "Thunder of the waters." The human habitations within sound of its fall were rare and far apart. Its few visitors came, gazed, and departed in silence and awe, having for their guide the child of the forest or the hardy backwoodsman. No staring, painted hotel rose over the woods and obtruded its pale face over the edge of the boiling river. The journey to it from the east was one of adventure and peril. The scarcely attainable shore of Goat Island, lying between the two great divisions of the cataract, had only been trodden by a few hardy adventurers, depending upon stout hearts and steady hands for escape from the imminent perils of the passage. How is it now? The forest has everywhere yielded to the axe. Hotels with their snug shrubberies, out-houses, gardens, and paltry establishments stare you in the face; museums, mills, staircases, tolls, and grog-shops, greet the eye of the traveler. Bridges are thrown from island to island; and Goat Island is reached without adventure.

But do not imagine that we grew peevish at the sight of the blots upon the landscape, to which I have alluded, and departed in wrath and disgust. We soon found that there was that in and about Niagara which was not to be marred by busy man and all his petty schemes for convenience and self-aggrandisement; and I may truly say, with regard to both our first and second visit, and stay within its precincts, that we were under the influence of its spell. While within the sound of its waters, I will not say you become part and parcel of the cataract, but you find it difficult to think, speak, or dream of any thing else. Its vibrations pervade, not only the air you breathe, the bank on which you sit, the paper on which you write, but thrill through your whole frame, and act upon your nervous system in a remarkable, and it may almost be said an unpleasant manner. You may have heard of people coming back from the contemplation of these Falls, with dissatisfied feelings. To me this is perfectly incomprehensible, and I do not know whether to envy the splendid fancies and expectations of that class of travellers, to whom the sight of Niagara would bring disappointment, or to feel justified in doubting whether they have any imagination or eye for natural scenery at all. How blank the world must be to them of objects of natural interest. What can they expect to see? As to expectations, ours were excited and warm, and I shall never forget the real anxiety with which we looked out, on our ascent from Lewistown, for the first appearance of the  object of our visit. The broad, fathomless blue river, streaked with foam, which, deeply sunk in a colossal channel, hurried to our rencontre, and appeared at every fresh glimpse as we advanced, swifter and in greater commotion, was to us a guarantee that the scene of its descent from the upper country could be no common one. When about three miles from the village on the American side, you gain your first view of the Falls, together with the river, both above and below,—the island, which divides them,—and greater part of the basin at their feet. I will not say but that the impression of that first glance was heightened afterward by our nearer and reiterated survey of every portion of the cataract in detail; yet we all agreed that we could even then grasp the idea of its magnitude, and that all we had seen elsewhere, and all we had expected, was far surpassed by what was then shown to us. And when, the following year, two of us turned aside by common consent to pay a second visit to Niagara, having in the interval, visited many of the great falls of Lower Canada,—cataracts in comparison to which all European Falls are puerile; and we felt our curiosity excited to divine what impression a second visit would make—far from being disappointed, we felt that before Niagara, in spite of its comparative inferiority of elevation, all shrunk to playthings. It is not the mere weight and volume of water that should give this far-famed cataract the first rank. Every surrounding object seems to be on a corresponding scale of magnificence. The wide liquid surface of the river above, with its luxuriantly verdure clad swelling banks, contrasted by the deep blue floods below, as, boiling up from their plunge, into the unfathomed basin they shock against one another, and race down toward the distant lake; the extreme beauty of the forested defile, with its precipices and slopes; the colorings of the water, which in the upper part of its descent, is that of the emerald; the mystery and thick gloom which hide the foot of the falls, and add to their apparent height, and the floating clouds of vapor, now hurried over the face of the landscape, as though urged by the breath of a hurricane, and then slowly ascending and hovering like a cloud in the blue sky, all combine to form a scene in which sublimity and picturesque beauty are enchantingly blended. There is here none of that stiffness either in the scenery, or the form and appearance of the particular object of interest, which engravings too frequently give you the idea of.

Among the innumerable points of view, that from the precipitous shore of the river, about the distance I have alluded to, is the most satisfactory, if not the most striking. In the immediate vicinity of the Falls, the points of interest are so various, that if you would require a sketch, I should not know which to select. The grandest, doubtless, is from the Canadian shore, near the Horse-Shoe Fall; but you pass from one to the other, and everywhere the picture presented has no compeer or rival in

nature. What a glorious scene! To sit upon the summit of the impending precipice of Goat Island, and see, as we did the morning after our first arrival, the summer mist begin to rise and disengage itself from the heavy white cloud of spray which rose from the depth of the boiling basin of the Great Fall beneath us. By degrees, the curtain was partially removed, revealing the wall of slowly-descending water behind, now dimly descried,—as, confounded with the floating sheets of foam and spray, which the wind of the mighty cataract drove backward and forward over it like innumerable clouds of thin floating gauze— it mocked us with its constantly varying shape and position; and then appearing unveiled with its sea-green tints, brilliantly illuminated by the passing sunbeam. An hour after and the mist had disappeared; the Falls were sparkling in the bright sunshine; and a brilliant Iris was resting on the body of vapor which the wind carried away from the face of the de-scending columns. The scene at sun-set, day after day, was no way less majestic, when the sun, glancing from the Canadian side of the river, lit up the precipices and woods of Goat Island, and the broad surface of the American Fall, which then glowed like a wall of gold; while half the Fall of the horse-shoe, and the deep recess of the curve were wrapped in deep shade. Morning, noon, and night, found us strolling about the shore and on the beautiful Island, which is an earthly paradise.

I remember the quiet hours spent there, when fatigued with the glare of the hot bright sun, and the din of the Falls, with peculiar delight. We loved, too, to escape from all those signs of man's presence, and busy-bodying to which I have alluded, and, burying ourselves in the fresh, dark, scarce-trodden forest still covering a great part of its area, to listen to the deadened roar of the vast cataracts on either hand, swelling on the air distinct from every other sound.

There, seated in comparative solitude, you catch a peep, across a long irregular vista of stems, of the white vapor and foam. You listen to the sharp cry of the blue jay, the tap of the red-headed woodpecker, and the playful bark of the squirrel; you scan the smooth white boles of the beech or birch, chequered with broad patches of dark-green moss, the stately elm and oak, the broad-leaved maple, the silvery white and exquisitely chiselled trunk of the cedar, or the decaying trunk of the huge chestnut, garlanded with creepers; but you will hardly ever lose the consciousness of the locality. The spell of Niagara is still upon and around you. You glance again and again at the white veil which thickens or grows dim beyond the leafy forest:—the rush of the nearer rapids, the din of falling waters, the murmur of the echoes answering the pulsations of the descending mass, fill your ears, and pervade all nature.

Every thing around and about you appears to reply to the Cataract, and to partake of it, none more so than the evergreen forest which is bathed from year to year in the dew of the river. These noble trees, as they tower aloft on the soil, are sustained from youth to age by the invigorating spray of the mighty Falls. Their leaves are steeped, summer after summer, in the heavy dew, their trunks echo the falling waters, from the day they rise from the sod, to that in which they are shaken to the ground; and the fibres of the huge moss-grown trunk, on which you sit, prostrate and mouldering on the rich mould beneath, bedded in the fresh grass and leaves, still vibrate to the sound of its thunders, and crumble gradually to dust. But all this proves nothing—as a matter-of-fact man might say—but that I am Niagara mad. Impelled by a passion for this variety of natural scenery, as a boy, there is something in the motion of a waterfall which always makes my brain spin with pleasure. We have much before us and many sublime scenes, though none may vie with that, before which we have been lingering:—*allons!*

A SYNCOPE OF THE WATERS.

GEORGE W. HOLLEY.

ON THE 20th of March, 1848, the river presented a remarkable phenomenon. There is no record of a similar one, nor has it been observed since. The winter had been intensely cold, and the ice formed on Lake Erie was very thick. This was loosened around the shores by the warm days of the early spring. During the day, a stiff easterly wind moved the whole field up the lake. About sundown, the wind chopped suddenly round and blew a gale from the west. This brought the vast tract of ice down again with such tremendous force that it filled in the neck of the lake and the outlet, so that the outflow of the water was very greatly impeded. Of course, it only needed a short space of time for the Falls to drain off the water below Black Rock. The consequence was that, when we arose in the morning at Niagara, we found our river was nearly half gone. The American channel had dwindled to a respectable creek. The British channel looked as though it had been smitten with a quick consumption, and was fast passing away. Far up from the head of Goat Island and out into the Canadian rapids the water was gone, as it was also from the lower end of Goat Island, out beyond the tower. The rocks were bare, black, and forbidding. The roar of Niagara had subsided almost to a moan. The scene was desolate, and but for its novelty and the certainty that it would change before many hours, would have been gloomy and saddening. Every person who has visited Niagara will remember a beautiful jet of water which shoots up into the air about forty rods south of the outer Sister in the great rapids, called, with a singular contradiction of terms, the "Leaping Rock." The writer drove a horse and buggy from near the head of Goat Island out to a point above and near to that jet. With a log-cart and four horses, he drew from the outside of the outer island a stick of pine timber hewed twelve inches square and forty feet long. From the top of the middle island was drawn a still larger stick, hewed on one side and sixty feet long.

There are few places on the globe where a person would be less likely to go lumbering than in the rapids of Niagara, just above the brink of the Horse-Shoe Fall. All the people of the neighborhood were abroad, exploring recesses and cavities that had never before been exposed to mortal eyes. The writer went some distance up the shore of the river. Large fields of the muddy bottom were laid bare. The shell-fish, the uni-valves, and the bi-valves were in despair. The clams, with their backs up and their open mouths down in the mud, were making their sinuous courses toward the shrunken stream. This singular syncope of the waters lasted all the day, and night closed over the strange scene. But in the morning our river was restored in all its strength and beauty and majesty.—*Falls of Niagara.*

GENERAL VIEW OF NIAGARA FALLS FROM PAINTING OF TEN COKE—IN 1831.
(Engraving in 1833 Given by Noah Brown.)

THE NIAGARA RIVER.

NIAGARA RIVER, which takes its name from the Falls, is thirty-six miles in length, reaching from Lake Erie to Lake Ontario. It receives the waters of all the upper lakes, viz., Erie, St. Clair, Huron, Michigan, Superior, and others smaller than these. St. Louis River, rising 1250 miles northwest of the Falls, and 150 miles west of Lake Superior, is the most remote source of this stream. Its position above the level of the sea is said to be 1200 feet, and in its course towards Lake Ontario, it makes a descent of 551 feet. The lakes and streams for which it is an outlet, cover an area of 150,000 square miles. The length of Lake Superior is 459 miles, its width 100 miles, and its depth 900 feet. The Straits of Saint Mary, 60 miles long, and 45 feet in its descent, conveys the waters of Lake Superior and Lake Huron, which receives also the waters of nearly forty rivers. Lake Michigan is 300 miles

OLD WINDMILL AT FORT ERIE.

long, 50 miles wide, and 900 feet deep. Its outlet is the Straits of Mackinac, conveying its waters into Lake Huron, a distance of 40 miles. Green Bay, formerly called the Bay of Puans, is on the northwest side of Lake Michigan, 100 miles long and 20 miles wide. Lake Huron is 218 miles in length, and 180 miles in width, and about 900 feet deep. Its waters flow into Lake Erie, through the Lake and River St. Clair, and the Detroit River, a distance of ninety miles, with a descent of 31 feet. Lake Erie is 290 miles long, 63 miles wide,

and 120 feet deep. Its level above the sea is 564 feet, and above Lake Ontario 334 feet, which, of course, is the descent it makes to the latter. The descent from Lake Erie, where the Niagara River commences, to Schlosser, is 12 feet; at the rapids it is 52 feet; at the Cataract 164 feet; from this point to Lewiston, 104 feet; thence to Lake Ontario, 2 feet. At Lake Erie, where the Niagara River commences, its width is about two miles; and its depth from 20 to 40 feet. At Black Rock it is narrowed

THE OUTLET OF NIAGARA RIVER—LAKE ONTARIO IN THE DISTANCE.
(Iroquois of old Kahkwahs.)

to a mile, and is, at that point, deep and rapid, moving at the rate of six or eight miles an hour. For three miles its current continues swift, and thence its course is slow, and its surface placid, until within one mile from the Falls. At the head of Grand Island, five miles from Lake Erie, it expands, and branches out into two streams, running on either side of this island, the greatest quantity of water flowing on the west side of the island, until it measures eight miles across. Below this, opposite Schlosser, it is nearly three miles in width, and appears smooth like the surface of a quiet lake. Its descent from this point to the Falls is 90 feet. At the Falls its width is three-quarters of a mile; at the Ferry it is 56 rods wide; at the Whirlpool 150 yards wide. Its depth varies, in different places, from 20 to 300 feet; and just below the Cataract it has never been fathomed. Niagara River embraces, in its course, many beautiful islands, the lesser ones of which are Bird Island, situated between Buffalo and Lake Erie; Square Island, opposite Black Rock, of

131 acres; Strawberry Island, of 100 acres; Beaver Island, of 30 acres; Rattlesnake Island, of 48 acres; Tonawanda Island, of 69 acres; Cayuga Island, of 100 acres, nearest to the American shore, four miles above the Falls; and Buck-horn Island, which is low and marshy, containing 146 acres. The two islands of principal note in this river, are Grand Island, of 17,384 acres, and Navy Island, of 304 acres.

The banks of Niagara River, from Fort Erie to the Canadian shore, at the outlet of Lake Erie, to Chippewa, a distance of eighteen miles, are from four to ten feet high. From Chippewa to the Falls themselves, a distance of two and a half miles, the bank is from ten to one hundred feet high, the descent of the river being ninety-two feet. From the Falls to Lewiston, a distance of seven miles, the bank varies from one hundred and fifty to three hundred feet. From Lewiston to Lake Ontario is seven miles, and in this distance the Northern Terrace, or Mountain Ridge, crosses the course of the river, when the banks diminish to twenty-five or thirty feet. The gorge through which the Niagara River flows, after leaving the precipice that forms the Cataract, "presents almost perpendicular walls, with a talus at the bottom, formed by the falling of some of the higher strata," says Hall, in the Geographical Survey of the State of New York. "The outlet of the chasm is scarcely wider than elsewhere along its course. In some places the channel is less than two hundred yards across, and again is extended to twice that width. The breadth of the chasm at the top is nearly twice as great as that of the stream below. The declivity of the bed of the river, from the Falls to Lewiston, is one hundred and four feet, or nearly fifteen feet in the mile.

"At one place, about a mile below the Falls, where the channel is narrowest, the stream glides with comparative stillness, while below this, where the channel is

broader, it is driven along with great velocity. Again, below the whirlpool, the surface of the river is more smooth, and the current more gentle, though the channel is narrower than above. In the course of this gorge, is a single exception to the parallel sides and nearly vertical cliffs; this is upon the west bank of the river at the whirlpool. The width of the gorge at Lewiston is 1500 or perhaps 2000 feet. In the Niagara chasm there are no boulders, pebbles or gravel. The river occupies the whole width, at the bottom, except a talus on either side, formed by angular fragments fallen from above.

"From all that appears along the present river course, there was probably an ancient shallow valley extending in the direction of the present Niagara River which gave the first direction to the waters."

DICKENS' NOTES.

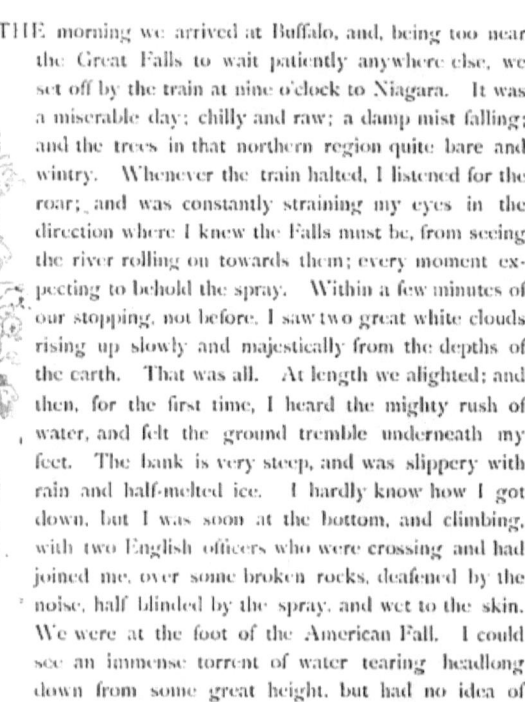

N THE morning we arrived at Buffalo, and, being too near the Great Falls to wait patiently anywhere else, we set off by the train at nine o'clock to Niagara. It was a miserable day; chilly and raw; a damp mist falling; and the trees in that northern region quite bare and wintry. Whenever the train halted, I listened for the roar; and was constantly straining my eyes in the direction where I knew the Falls must be, from seeing the river rolling on towards them; every moment expecting to behold the spray. Within a few minutes of our stopping, not before, I saw two great white clouds rising up slowly and majestically from the depths of the earth. That was all. At length we alighted; and then, for the first time, I heard the mighty rush of water, and felt the ground tremble underneath my feet. The bank is very steep, and was slippery with rain and half-melted ice. I hardly know how I got down, but I was soon at the bottom, and climbing, with two English officers who were crossing and had joined me, over some broken rocks, deafened by the noise, half blinded by the spray, and wet to the skin. We were at the foot of the American Fall. I could see an immense torrent of water tearing headlong down from some great height, but had no idea of shape, or situation, or anything but vague immensity. When we were seated in the little ferry-boat, and were crossing the swollen river, immediately before both cataracts, I began to feel what it was; but I was in a manner stunned, and unable to comprehend the vastness of the scene. It was not until I came on Table Rock, and looked—Great Heaven, on what a fall of bright green water!—that it came upon me in its full might and majesty.

Then, when I felt how near to my Creator I was standing, the first effect, and the enduring one—instant and lasting—of the tremendous spectacle, was Peace. Peace of Mind, tranquility, calm recollections of the Dead, great thoughts of Eternal Rest and Happiness; nothing of gloom or terror. Niagara was at once stamped upon my heart, an Image of Beauty; to remain there, changeless and indelible, until its pulses cease to beat, for ever.

ROCK OF AGES AND CAVE OF THE WINDS.

Oh, how the strife and trouble of daily life receded from my view, and lessened in the distance, during the ten memorable days we passed on that Enchanted Ground! What voices spoke from out the thundering water; what faces, faded from the earth, looked out upon me from its gleaming depths; what Heavenly promise glistened in those angel's tears, the drops of many hues, that showered around, and twined themselves about the gorgeous arches which the changing rainbows made!

I never stirred in all that time from the Canadian side, whither I had gone at first. I never crossed the river again; for I knew there were people on the other shore, and in such a place it is natural to shun strange company. To wander to and fro all day, and see the cataracts from all points of view; to stand upon the edge of the Great Horse-Shoe Fall, marking the hurried water gathering strength as it approached the verge, yet seeming, too, to pause before it shot into the gulf below; to gaze from the river's level up at the torrent as it came streaming down; to climb the neighboring heights and watch it through the trees, and see the wreathing water in the rapids hurrying on to take its fearful plunge; to linger in the shadow of the solemn rocks three miles below; watching the river as, stirred by no visible cause, it heaved and eddied and awoke the echoes, being troubled yet, far down beneath the surface, by its giant leap; to have Niagara before me lighted by the sun and by the moon, red in the day's decline, and grey as evening slowly fell upon it; to look upon it every day, and wake up in the night and hear its ceaseless voice; this was enough.

I think in every quiet season now, still do those waters roll and leap, and roar and tumble, all day long; still are the rainbows spanning them, a hundred feet below. Still, when the sun is on them, do they shine and glow like molten gold. Still, when the day is gloomy, do they fall like snow, or seem to crumble away like the front of a great chalk cliff, or roll down the rock like dense white smoke. But always does the mighty stream appear to die as it comes down, and always from its unfathomable grave arises that tremendous ghost of spray and mist, which is never laid; which has haunted this place with the same dread solemnity since Darkness brooded on the deep, and that first flood before the Deluge — Light — came rushing on Creation at the word of God.

BURNING OF THE CAROLINE.

An Incident of the Patriot War in 1837.

OF ALL the places in the world for a naval engagement the head of the Upper Rapids of the Niagara River would seem to be the last one chosen. The necessities of war, however, brought about a miniature battle in the immediate vicinity of the raging waters. Mr. H. T. Allen in his guide to Niagara Falls gives an excellent version of the affair, well worthy of preservation as a reliable page of modern history.

"In 1837, a rebellion was stirred up against the authorities of Canada, by some disaffected 'Radicals,' under the leadership of Wm. Lyon McKenzie and some others; but, Her Majesty's subjects not caring to side with the 'Rebels' in any great number, the movement was speedily put down. But not so the leaders. They—*i. e.* McKenzie, Gen. Sutherland, and five and six and twenty others—at the suggestion of Dr. Chapin, of Buffalo, unfurled the standard of rebellion over Navy Island, designing to make it a *rendez-vous* for the restless patriots of both sides of the river, until sufficient strength should be gained to renew the attack. Matters were going on pleasantly—the 'Patriots' being daily edified by accessions to their strength, though greatly demoralized by a barrel of whiskey that found its way to their panting hearts—when the difficulty of transporting volunteers and supplies to their place of destination, and the number of persons, from motives of business or curiosity, constantly desirous of passing and repassing from the main-land to the patriot camp, suggested to Mr. Wells, the owner of a small steamboat lying at Buffalo, called the Caroline, the idea of taking out the necessary papers, and running his vessel as a ferry boat between the American shore and the island, for his own pecuniary emolument. Accordingly, Friday, December 29, the Caroline left Buffalo for Schlosser; and after having arrived, having made several trips during the day, on account of the owner, was moored to the wharf at Schlosser Landing during the night.

"Colonel Allan McNab, then commanding at Chippewa a detachment of Her Majesty's forces, having got word of the enterprise of the Caroline, resolved upon a deed which relieves the farcical story of the rebellion by a dash of genuine daring. It is asserted that Sir Allan was informed that the Caroline was in the interests of the Patriots, chartered for their use, and intended to act offensively against the Canadian authorities. Whether this be true or not, he planned her destruction that very night. For this purpose a chosen band was detailed and placed under the command of Captain Drew, a retired-on-half-pay officer, of the royal navy.

"At midnight, the captain received his parting orders from Sir Allan, and the chivalrous band departed in eight boats for the scene of their gallant daring.

"The unconscious Caroline, meanwhile lay peacefully at her moorings, beneath the stars and stripes of her country's banner. As the tavern at Schlosser—the only building near by—could accommodate but a limited number of persons, several had sought a night's lodging within the sides of the boat. Dreaming of no danger, they had retired to rest unprovided with arms. Thus was the night wearing on, when so stealthily came the hostile band that the faint splash of muffled oars was the first intimation that the sentry had of their approach. In reply to his question, 'Who goes there?' came, first '*Friends!*' then a heavy plashing in the water; then, the leaping of armed men to the deck. The bewildered sleepers start from their dreams and rush for the shore. 'Cut them down!' shrieks the heroic Drew, as he thrills with the memory of Abóukir and Nile—'Cut them down, give no quarter.' More or less injured, they escape to the shore, with life—all but one, Durfee, the last man to leave, who is brought to the earth by a pistol shot, a corpse! A few minutes and the Caroline moves from the shore in flames! Down the wild current she speeds, faster and faster, flinging flames in her track, till striking the Canada waters she spurns the contact, leaps like a mad fury, and in a moment more is as dark as the night around her. The common account of this affair takes it for granted that the boat went over the Canada Falls aflame. You will read of the fated vessel lifting her fairy form to the verge of the precipice, lighting up the dark amphitheatre of cataracts, etc., to the end of endurance. The case was far otherwise. The physician who was called to the wounded at Schlosser was riding up the river's bank while the Caroline was descending the rapids. The gentleman testifies that the boat, a perfect mass of illumination, her timbers all aflame, and her pipes red hot, instantly expired when she struck the cascade below the head of Goat Island." This was a crushing blow to the rebellion.

BURNT SHIP BAY is called from a circumstance connected with the close of the French war of 1759. The garrison at Schlosser had already made a gallant resistance to one attack of the English and were preparing for another, when, disheartened by the news of the fall of Quebec, they resolved to destroy the two armed vessels containing their military stores. Accordingly they brought them to this bay and set them on fire. The wrecks, even at this day, are sometimes visible.

SHADOW OF THE ROCK AND INCLINED RAILWAY.

HOW TO SEE THE CATARACT.

J. B. HARRISON.

IS IT worth while to report and describe truly the existing conditions at Niagara Falls? Thoughtful people find this a place of wonderful interest, of unparalleled attraction; yet some of their most vivid impressions and remembrances of the spot are eminently unsatisfactory and disagreeable. The scenery here has an absolutely exhaustless vitality. Its beauty grows upon every observer who remains long enough to recognize the truth that the spectacle upon which he gazes is never twice the same. The longer one studies the view at some points the more unwilling he is to turn away. It is like leaving a play of entrancing interest which has not yet ended. And here the play never ends. This is the great characteristic of Niagara,—its "infinite variety." There are several places in the rapids, and especially about the head of Goat Island, at each of which the changing show of the forms and motions of the water,—flinging, tossing, flying, exploding, thrown high into the air in great revolving bands and zones of crystal drops, shooting aloft in slender, vertical jets of feathery spray, swinging in wide-based, massive waves like those of the ocean, or gathered into billows which forever break and fall in curving cascades, and yet seem not to fall because they are every moment renewed, —are worth a journey across the continent to see.

FOUR SEPARATE WATERFALLS.

There is a great variety of beauty and interest even in the Falls themselves. As Luna Island divides the American Fall, making a beautiful separate cascade of the narrow stream which runs next to Goat Island, so the small island called Terrapin Rocks (on which Terrapin Tower formerly stood) cuts off a broader portion of the stream on the Canadian side of Goat Island, and makes a separate cataract there. Thus, when the spectator is on the lower end of Goat Island, there is on each side of him, first, a narrow strait or portion of the river, just large enough to form a fine fall by itself, then a small island, and further on a great cataract,—the American Fall on one side and the Horse-Shoe Fall on the other. These divisions of the stream, with four separate waterfalls, different in volume and environment, and so each possessing a marked individuality of character, yet so related to each other that they may be regarded as forming two great falls, and also as constituting, when all taken together the one great cataract of Niagara,— render the scene far more beautiful and interesting than one great fall of the undivided river could possibly be; while the fact that the height of the fall is everywhere very nearly the same maintains the impression of a complete and all-encompassing unity in the central spectacle of the place.

FORT NIAGARA IN 1844.

There is great variety, again, in the lines of the curves made by the descending water as it leaves the brink of the fall, as an artist would at once observe, and some of these curves are wonderfully majestic and beautiful. There are also many different curves and irregular variations in the line of the top or brow of the precipice over which the water rolls; and while for the most part the water falls sheer and free from the edge of the cliff till it strikes the stones at the bottom, there are in some places projecting rocks a little way below the top of the fall, upon which the descending stream is broken, and from which it is thrown for the rest of the way down into new lines of movement and new forms of beauty, thus adding another element of variety to the face of the cataract. In some places the stream pours with a steady roar into soundless depths of water at the foot of the precipice; in others it dashes with indescribable violence upon great masses of rock below, from which it is hurled outward with terrific force in hissing streams and spouts of spray. The color of the falling water also varies everywhere. It is of snowy, dazzling whiteness where the current is shallow above, and the descending stream consequently thin. There is a little green mingled with the white where the volume of water is some-

what greater, and in the central portions of the Great or Horse-Shoe Fall the deep, intense, solid green of the water has a wonderful vitality and beauty. The magnificent framework of green foliage in which this glorious spectacle of the myriad forms and shows of moving water—from the wild, gay tossing of the rapids to the solemn fall of the cataract—is set, is an essential and indispensable part of its interest and loveliness. The massive growth of trees and enveloping vine canopies on the islands and river shore give to the scene such sylvan aspects of grace, of softness and tenderness, as constitute some of the chief elements in its unspeakable charm, and some of the most forceful qualities by which it makes its eternal appeal to the heart of man. Niagara would not be what it is now if it rolled through a bare, brown desert of limestone. It is not the water—the river—alone that gives to the place its unequalled attraction, its companionless grandeur and loveliness. If the trees should be destroyed, and the shores and islands denuded of their green and living beauty, the waters might rush and leap in the rapids, and roll over the cliff into the gulf below, as now; but our sense of their sparkling gladness and gayety, and of the tenderness and passionate, eager youthfulness in the life of the scene would be gone. The sentiment of the place, and the thoughts and feelings appealed to and inspired by it, would be wholly different from what they are now; and they would necessarily be of a much lower order and of a less vital quality. The value of this scenery, as a great possession for the human spirit, a source of uplifting, vivifying inspiration for those who can receive and enjoy such influences, would be terribly, fatally impaired.

WHY SOME PERSONS ARE DISAPPOINTED.

Some people do not see or feel, in any considerable degree, the spiritual charm of which I speak. They would not think of coming to Niagara for reinforcement of strength, for soothing, healing delights, or uplifting peace, or for help of any kind for the deeper needs of this life. They come hither because it is the fashion; the place lies in the round of travel, and they sit in their carriages at the top of the stairway leading down to Terrapin Rocks and look at the Great Fall for a minute and a half, and usually remark, as they pass onward, that it is a less curious and interesting spectacle than they had expected to see, and that, "on the whole," Niagara disappoints them. Of course it disappoints, and must forever disappoint, all who look at it in this foolish, hurried way. It requires time for the faculties of the human mind to be put in motion, and to respond to such a spectacle as this. Nay, it takes time even for the senses to recognize its most obvious material forms and aspects, and such persons do not give themselves time even for that. "May be I can't appreciate it as some can," they say. No; they might, in a minute and a half, "appreciate" the burst of colored fire from a sky-rocket, and enjoy its value to the full; and they do not understand that Niagara is a spectacle of another order. Unless they can become more thoughtful, the scene here is not for them.

There are other people to whom Niagara means much. It offers to those who are weary from toil of any kind, of hand or brain, or from the wearing, exhausting quality which is so marked in modern life,—it offers to all such a vital change, the relief and benefit of new scenes and new mental activities and experiences consequent upon observing them and becoming interested in them. Then, for those who will give time and opportunity for the scene to make its appeal, time for their minds to respond to its influences, there is something deeper and higher than this. There is a quickening and uplifting of the higher powers of the mind, an awakening of the imagination; the soul expands and aspires, rising to the level of a new and mighty companionship. Self-respect becomes more vital. Good things seem nearer and more real, and the nobleness and worth which but now we thought beyond attainment by us appear part of our inheritance as children of the Highest. I am not concerned to indicate the different ways in which the sentiment or spirit of the scenery, revealed through its local aspects and characteristics of infinitely varied grandeur and beauty, at last opens communication between itself and what is highest and most vital in the mind and heart of man. It is little worth while to try very hard to enjoy or appreciate Niagara. It is worth while to try to see, to become well acquainted with the form and appearance of each particular scene and part of the landscape, especially along the rapids and river shores, and about the falls as seen from above; and then, without any straining after high feeling or raptures of any kind, one is likely, by and by, to have a sense that the visit to Niagara has been a deep and vital experience, and that the place has become a real resource and possession to the soul forever. It is easy to write too much and too particularly of all this; for such experiences and feelings, like all the higher moods and activities of the soul, have something shy and elusive about them, and it is not often best to try to describe them. And Niagara itself, in its sovereign dignity and perfection, shames and silences all effort at description or eulogy. It is to be seen, felt—not talked about. And as the weeks and months pass while I dwell here, by the very shrine of this awful beauty, this veiled and shrouded grandeur, I become more and more unwilling to write about it, and can well believe that if one remained here long, all attempts at expression regarding it would appear inappropriate and futile, and that silence would seem the only true tribute. Perhaps a great artist might feel an unappeasable longing to express his feelings upon canvas,—if, indeed, the scene is not too great to be painted.

MISUSED OPPORTUNITIES.

But I write of Niagara for two reasons: one is, that so many people, who ought to have pleasure and delight in seeing it, now come here and go away without having felt delight at all,—go away, in fact, with feelings of disappointment and vexation, which settle at last into a decided impression and permanent remembrance of Niagara as a disagreeable place. In a great many cases this might be wholly or in a very great measure prevented; and it is for this reason, and not at all for the sake of any attempt at description, that I write on this subject. Most of the people who come hither are possessed of but moderate means to sustain the expenses of travel for pleasure or recreation, and, in consequence, they can remain at the Falls but a short time. Now, this is the class of persons who most need, and should be able in greatest degree to enjoy, whatever delights or benefits the place can minister to its visitors. The rich are better able to take care of themselves, here as everywhere. Or, if they do not know how to enjoy Niagara, they are able to stay long enough to learn. But thousands come hither for whom a day, or two days, is all the time that can be devoted to this experience. If people will manage wisely it is worth while to travel five hundred miles to see Niagara, even if they can remain

AMERICAN RAPIDS, FROM BATH ISLAND.

here but six hours. Most people who are here but for a day or two throw away the larger part of their time, so limited and precious, and lose the real opportunities of the visit almost wholly. They go to the wrong places, and do the wrong things, and so waste not only their time but their money. If one can be here but six or eight hours, he should not think of using a hack or carriage. He should walk. And any woman who can walk two miles at home can see Niagara, can see all there is essential or important here, without troubling a hack-driver or being troubled by him. If women would but bring with them a pair of comfortable shoes, already somewhat worn, and put on clothing that is reasonably light and loose, for the day, they could easily walk wherever it is necessary for short-time visitors to go.

PROSPECT PARK. The proper place to be first visited by all intelligent persons is the point at the top of the American Fall, on the American or village side of the river This place is included in 'Prospect Park,' and twenty-five cents is charged for admission at the gate. It is much to be regretted that there is now no point from which an inhabitant of our country can see Niagara Falls without the payment of a fee. But it is a fact, and visitors, must, of course, accept existing conditions and conform to them. The evil is not one for which any individual persons are to be blamed. It is inseparable from the personal ownership of the valuable land adjacent to the river at this point. The land here should have remained permanently the property of the State or of the National Government; and if the State should reacquire the title to all the land which is essential to the scenery of Niagara, it would be a most wise and benificent measure, and would, no doubt, tend in an appreciable degree to national advancement in civilization. The view of the American Fall from this point, of the river below, and of Goat Island and part of the Horse-Shoe Fall beyond it, is naturally the first in an ascending series which includes all that is indispensable or even very important to the visitor. There are comfortable seats in the park, the place is pleasant enough in the daytime, and the view all that can be desired from one place. But it is just here that foolish waste of time and money on the part of the short time visitor usually begins. There is a railway down an inclined plane through the bank to the river below; there are guides, and dressing-rooms, and water-proof suits, and all sorts of appropriate arrangements down there for creeping around, as a moist, unpleasant body, in a blinding storm of spray about the foot of the fall, and in "The Shadow of the Rock," where there is nothing of interest to be seen, and where, if there were untellable wonders, nobody could see them. Here at Niagara, where the fees are heaviest, the "sights" have least interest and value.

GOAT ISLAND.

Everybody appears to be specially interested in having you visit these places, where it is all feeling and no seeing; but the intelligent short-time visitor will say

THE HERMIT'S CASCADE.

no, in a way to be understood, and, leaving the Park by the gate nearest the river, will walk a few rods up the stream (by the very edge of the American Rapids) to Goat Island Bridge. Here the fee is fifty cents. (If you are to remain for some days, pay one dollar here and seventy-five cents at Prospect Park, and come and go at your pleasure without further charge.) At the island end of the bridge take the steps up the bank to the right. A beautifully shaded walk through the forest brings you to Luna Island, at the top and very edge of the American Fall on that side. When ready to proceed keep to the right from the top of the stairway, by a pleasant path along the edge of the island, pausing at various points for characteristic views, but not pausing for the descent to the "Cave of the Winds," where there are more dressing-rooms, more rubber suits, more guides, more soaking, dashing mists, etc., requiring time and money in proportion. The walk to the Great Fall requires but a few moments. Look at it first from the head of the stairway, then from Terrapin Rocks (where Terrapin Tower formerly stood).

THE RAPIDS.

You must not think you have seen Niagara because you have seen the Falls. The Rapids at the head of Goat Island, and the varied and wonderful scenery of the "Three Sisters" at that point—all this is indispensable. You have not seen Niagara if you have omitted this region. It is but a few minutes' walk again, still keeping to the right along the edge of the island after you leave the Great Fall. Leaving the "Three Sisters," go directly across the carriage road, up the steps and past the excursion or picnic building in the woods, passing to the right of it. A

broad path through the woods leads to the end of the bridge by which you crossed to Goat Island. Having paid your half-dollar to go to the island, every point and prospect upon it and around it is free to you. There are no further fees.

And now, if one has followed the course here indicated, spending, of course, as much time as he can afford at the different points of interest, and especially in the solitudes of the islands, he may rightly feel he has seen Niagara, or that he has been at the right places for seeing what is essential to the charm and wonder of the place, so far as it is possible to see and feel it in so short a time. There have been but two fees, amounting to 75 cts. If the visitor must leave now, he need not think with much regret of what he has not seen. If he can stay longer, the next thing is to cross the new suspension bridge into Canada. The fee on the bridge is 25 cts. each way. The view of the Falls from the Canada side is free.—*N. Y. Evening Post.*

CANADIAN RAPIDS ABOVE THE FALLS.

A LAST LOOK.

J. S. BUCKINGHAM.

ON THE following morning we went to take a last look of the Falls before quitting them perhaps forever, and we all agreed that our sensations at the last view were as powerful as at the first. For my own part, I do not think it would be possible for any number of repetitions in the view to take away, or even abate, the first impression produced by the richness, splendor, magnificence, and sublimity of this great and glorious object of nature. To the many who visit this spot without a taste for the grand or beautiful—and to the extent of their numbers the register at the Table Rock produces painful evidence—I can understand its becoming tiresome; but to those whose feelings harmonize with the sublime objects that are here combined and presented to the wondering view, I cannot comprehend how they should be otherwise than enchanted from first to last, and impressed with all the sensations of pleasure, admiration, triumph, and devotion in succession.

The sunlights were more varied to-day than we had observed them to be on any preceding visit, and this is a powerful cause of variety in the appearance of the Falls. There were passing clouds that occasionally obscured the sun, when deep shadows overhung the waters. Suddenly the bright orb would burst forth from its hiding-place, and in an instant the whole mass was lighted up with luminous and transparent brilliancy. Occasional showers of rain also fell, and the rainbows of the spray seemed to look more than usually vivid and glowing. The smooth deep current between the turbulent rapids of the upper strait and the immediate edge of the cataract flowed on like a stream of molten glass, so clear, so lucid, and yet so unwrinkled in its surface, that when it curved over the brink of the precipice, the mass poured downward was like a liquid emerald of the brightest and most transparent green. As this was varied with the sparkling lights of the broken waters, it resembled those beautiful glimpses which the mariner sometimes catches of the mountain wave at sea, when the lustre of the setting sun is seen through its upper edge of the brightest green, and a curling wave of the whitest foam crowns its towering and majestic crest. The whole seemed to realize the splendid imagery of Milton, in his exquisite description of the

> "Throne of royal state, which far
> Outshone the wealth of Ormus or of Ind,
> Or where the gorgeous East, with richest hand,
> Showers on her kings barbaric pearls and gold."

I have seen no other object in nature, in all my various wanderings, equal this in magnificence and sublimity. The impression of its beauty and grandeur is so deeply imprinted on my heart and mind, that I am sure I shall carry it with me to the grave, if reason and memory are spared to me till then.

THE RAPIDS AND GORGE.

GEORGE KNIGHTON.

THE UPPER RAPIDS.

STILL, with the wonder of boyhood, I follow the race of the Rapids,
Sirens that dance, and allure to destruction,—now lurking in shadows,
Skirting the level stillness of pools and the treacherous shallows,
Smiling and dimple-mouthed, coquetting,—now modest, now forward;

Tenderly chanting, and such the thrall of the weird incantation,
Thirst it awakes in each listener's soul, a feverish longing,
Thoughts all-absorbent, a torment that stings and ever increases,
Burning ambition to push bare-breast to thy perilous bosom.

Thus, in some midnight obscure, bent down by the storm of temptation
(So hath the wind, in the beechen wood, confided the story),
Pine-trees, thrusting their way and trampling down one another,
Curious, lean and listen, replying in sobs and in whispers;

Tall of the secret possessed, which brings sure blight to the hearer,
(So hath the wind, in the beechen wood, confided the story),
Faltering, they stagger brinkward,—clutch at the roots of the grasses,
Cry,—a pitiful cry of remorse,—and plunge down in the darkness.

Art thou all-merciless then,—a fiend, ever fierce for new victims?
Was then the red-man right (as yet it liveth in legend),
That, ere each twelvemonth circles, still to thy shrine is allotted
Blood of one human heart, as sacrifice due and demanded?

Butterflies have I followed, that leaving the red-top and clover,
Thinking a wind-harp thy voice, thy froth the fresh whiteness of daisies,
Ventured too close, grew giddy, and catching cold drops on their pinions,
Balanced—but vainly,—and falling, their scarlet was blotted forever.

THE GORGE.

NEATH the abyss lies the Valley, a valley of darkness,—a hades,
Where the spent stream, as it strives, seeks only an end to its anguish;
Who shall its fastnesses fathom, or tell what wrecks they envelop?
Here 'neath the tides of time, life's remnants await resurrection.

Deep is the way, and weary the way, while lofty above it
Frowns, upon either hand, a cliff sheer-shouldered or beetling,
Holding in durance forever the corpse of the will broken exile,
Blighting all hope of return, should it pant for the flowering pastures.

But from the brinks lean down a few slender birches and cedars,
Dazed by the depth and the gloom of the channels resounding beneath them;
Here campanulas, too, which lurk wherever is danger,
Stoop with a smile of hope, reflecting the blue of the heavens.

Fleeter still flies the flood, up-heaping its scum at the centre,
Dragging the tides from the shores to leave them a hand-breadth the lower;
While, like a serpent of yellow, the spume crooks down to the Whirlpool,
Trails with a zigzagging motion down to the hideous Whirlpool.

THE PIN-RA-VEL AND MANITOU ROCK

THE MAID OF THE MIST.

ONE OF THE most daring feats ever accomplished successfully by man was that of the navigation of the Whirlpool Rapids, thence through the dreadful whirlpool to Lake Ontario, with the little steamer "Maid of the Mist." Mr. Geo. W. Holley, himself an old resident of Niagara Falls, in his late work on Niagara Falls, gives a very interesting account of the little boat, her pilot and her trip, rendered more valuable through the personal acquaintance of the author with the actors in the thrilling undertaking. He says: "In the year 1846, a small steamer was built in the eddy just above the Railway Suspension Bridge, to run up to the Falls. She was very appropriately named 'The Maid of the Mist.' Her engine was rather weak, but she safely accomplished the trip. As, however, she took passengers aboard only from the Canadian side, she could pay little more than expenses. In 1854 a larger, better boat, with a more powerful engine, the new 'Maid of the Mist,' was put on the route, and as she took passengers from both sides of the river, many thousands of persons made the exciting and impressive voyage up to the Falls. The admiration which the visitor felt as he passed quietly along near the American Fall was changed into awe when he began to feel the mighty pulse of the great deep just below the tower, then swung round into the white foam directly in front of the Horse-Shoe, and saw the sky of waters falling toward him. And he seemed to be lifted on wings as he sailed swiftly down on the rushing stream through a baptism of spray. To many persons there was a fascination about it that induced them to make the trip every time they had an opportunity to do so. Owing to some change in her appointments which confined her to the Canadian shore for the reception of passengers, she became unprofitable. Her owner, having decided to leave the neighborhood, wished to sell her as she lay at her dock. This he could not do, but he received an offer of something more than half of her cost, if he would deliver her at Niagara, opposite the fort. This he decided to do, after consultation with Robinson, who had acted as her captain and pilot on her trips below the Falls. Mr. Robinson agreed to act as pilot for the fearful voyage, and the engineer, Mr. Jones, consented to go with him. A courageous machinist, Mr. McIntyre, volunteered to share the risk with them. They put her in complete trim, removing from deck and hold all superfluous articles. Notice was given of the time for starting, and a large number of people assembled to see the fearful plunge, no one expecting to see the crew again alive after they should leave the dock, just above the Railway Suspension Bridge. Twenty rods below, the water plunges sharply down into the head of the crooked, tumultuous rapid, reaching from the bridge to the Whirlpool. At the Whirlpool, the danger of being drawn under was most to be apprehended; in the rapids, of being turned over or knocked to pieces. From the Whirlpool to Lewiston is one wild, turbulent rush and whirl of water, without a square foot of smooth surface in the whole distance.

"About three o'clock in the afternoon of June 15, 1861, the engineer took his place in the hold, and, knowing that their flitting would be short at the best, and might be only the preface to swift destruction, set his steam valve at the proper gauge, and awaited—not without anxiety—the tinkling signal that should start them on their flying voyage. McIntyre joined Robinson at the wheel on the upper deck. Self-possessed, and with the calmness which results from undoubting courage and confidence, yet with the humility which recognizes all possibilities, with downcast eyes and firm hands, Robinson took his place at the wheel and pulled the starting bell. With a shriek from her whistle and a white puff from her escape pipe, the boat ran up the eddy a short distance, then swung round to the right, cleared the smooth water, and shot like an arrow into the rapid under the bridge. Robinson intended to take the inside curve of the rapid, but a fierce cross-current carried him to the outer-curve, and when a third of the way down it a jet of water struck against her rudder, a column dashed up under her starboard side, heeled her over, carried away her smoke-stack, started her overhang on that side, threw Robinson flat on his back, and thrust McIntyre against her starboard wheel-house with such force as to break it through. Every eye was fixed, every tongue was silent, and every looker on breathed freer as she emerged from the fearful baptism, shook her wounded sides, slid into the Whirlpool, and for a moment rode again on an even keel. Robinson rose at once, seized the helm, and set her to the right of the large pot in the pool, then turned her directly through the neck of it. Thence, after receiving another drenching from its combing waves, she dashed on without further accident, to the quiet bosom of the river below Lewiston. Thus was accomplished one of the most remarkable and perilous voyages ever made by men.

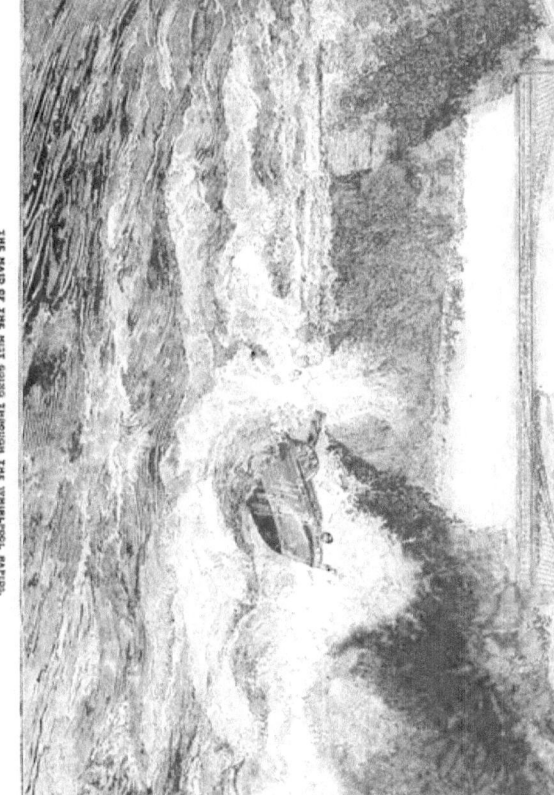

"THE MAID OF THE MIST GOING THROUGH THE WHIRLPOOL RAPIDS."

THE CATARACT.

FORMING the Cataract of Niagara are three separate Falls, produced by the intervention of islands dividing the river in its descending course, and presenting, on their southern sides, high precipices, the extension of which forms the area of descent. That portion of the torrent which is between Goat and Luna Islands, is called the Central Fall. Between the American shore and Luna Island is the American Fall; and the British or Horse-Shoe Fall, between Goat Island and the Canadian shore. The two former Cascades viewed together are usually called the American Fall, and have a descent of one hundred and sixty-four feet; they stretch to an extent of one thousand feet. The Horse-Shoe Fall is the largest portion of the Cataract, having an extent of two thousand and one hundred feet, and a height of one hundred and fifty-eight feet. Its shape is more like an Indian bow than a horse shoe, the curve of which, in its center, is always obscured by the clouds of vapor that ascend from the turbulent tide below. The water is precipitated over a ledge of rocks in a compact mass into a chasm, the depth of which has never been correctly ascertained. From the violence and rapidity of the water below, all efforts to fathom it have been vain; but it is supposed to be about two hundred and forty feet deep.

Various attempts have been made to arrive at a correct estimate of the amount of water passing over the precipice of Niagara. Dr. Dwight, taking the depth, width, and velocity of the current, as his data, calculated that more than eighty-five millions of tons went over per hour. By another calculation, supposing the current to run at the rate of six miles per hour, instead of five as in the first, the quantity has been estimated at the rate of 102,093,750 tons per hour. But this estimate of the velocity of the tide is regarded as too high, a point however which can scarcely be decided upon from the fierceness and force of the falling torrent. The following table of calculations respecting the amount of water flowing down the Niagara river, is taken from the Geological Survey of the State of New York.

By Dr. Dwight, it is estimated at	31,492,742 cubic feet per minute.
By Mr. Darby, " " "	27,878,400 " "
By Mr. Pickens, " "	18,087,533 " "
By Mr. Barrett, " "	19,500,000 " "

The last estimate is from three different observations made at Black Rock. The extremes of all the observations did not vary more than 20,000 feet per minute. It will be seen from the variations in the foregoing calculations that a correct estimate can scarcely be arrived at upon this point. A general idea therefore only may be gained of the immense quantity of water that flows so uninterruptedly at these Falls. This idea may be more fully impressed upon the mind, by considering also the fact, that the lakes and tributary streams supplying the river Niagara, cover a surface of about one hundred and fifty thousand square miles; the land surface drained by them measuring nearly half a million of square miles. The spray arising from this immense mass of falling water is always ascending, and visible in moving columns, except when scattered by the winds. It assumes a pyramidal form, and passes off into clouds that hover over the point from which it ascends, and is seen at great distance.

The grandest view of every shade of color included in the rainbow, may be seen by the morning's sun above the Falls. From the head of the rapids, as near the Falls as possible, gigantic clouds of mists are seen arising at the edge of the cataract. In passing slowly over, with the sun several hours high at your back, every conceivable hue of the colors of the rainbow can be examined in turn, at leisure, a sight which would dazzle an artist with a specimen of nature's painting hard to imitate.

THE NEW SUSPENSION BRIDGE.

THIS ELEGANT structure was completed in 1869, and is located some 300 yards below the American Falls. It is 1268 feet in length, and calculated only for a carriage way and foot walk. The height of the bridge above the river is 190 feet and the towers at each end are over 100 feet high. These are provided with suitable stairways and elevators to reach the top, from which fine views of the scenery can be had. The bridge is undisturbed by ordinary winds; but winds that are but gentle breezes on the land, strike the bridge with the force of a brisk gale, and a gale on land becomes a storm on the water. The winds press through the gorge as through a funnel. Even in calm weather, puffs of wind come up from the Falls, surcharged with spray, and then, there may be seen, in sunshine, the new phenomenon of a rainbow, both over and under the platform, describing a complete circle round about the bridge.

One of America's foremost writers, whose works have probably ministered a pure and wholesome delight to a greater number of readers than those of any other American author, Howells, describes, in his history of a certain wedding journey to Niagara Falls, the superb view from this bridge. "The last hues of sunset lingered in the mists that sprung from the base of the Falls with a mournful, tremulous grace, and a movement weird as the play of the Northern Lights. They were touched with the most delicate purples and crimsons, that darkened to deep red, and then faded from them at a second look, and they flew upward, swiftly upward, like troops of pale, transparent ghosts; while a perfectly clear radiance, better than any other for local color, dwelt upon the scene. Far under the bridge the river smoothly ran, the undercurrents forever unfolding themselves upon the surface with a vast roselike evolution, edged all round with faint lines of white, where the air that filled the water freed itself in foam. What had been clear green on the face of the cataract was here more like rich verd antique, and had a look of firmness almost like that of the stone itself. So it showed beneath the bridge, and down the river till the curving shores hid it. These, springing abruptly from the water's brink, and shagged with pine and cedar, displayed the tender verdure of grass and bushes intermingled with the dark evergreens that climb from ledge to ledge, till they point their speary tops above the crest of the bluffs. In front, where tumbled rocks and expanses of naked clay varied the gloomier and gayer green, sprung those spectral mists; and through them loomed out, in its manifold majesty, Niagara, with the seemingly immovable, white Gothic screen of the American Fall, and the green massive curve of the Horse-Shoe, solid and simple and calm as an Egyptian wall; while behind this, with their white and black expanses broken by dark foliaged little isles, the steep Canadian rapids billowed down between their heavily wooded shores."

THE SPIRIT OF THE FALLS.

FROM CITY TO CATARACT.

FROM Toronto we steam across the lake to the village of Niagara, where a train is waiting to carry us on to the falls about half an hour further on. We all watch from the windows, eager to catch our first glimpse of the world's great wonder. We feel a nervous anxiety to stand in its majestic presence. I quote from my companion's note-book on the spot. "There was a break in the wood, a flash of white, a cloud of spray tossed high above the tree-tops; then the dark woods closed again. That glimpse, flashing upon us and passing before we could fully realize that the great tumbling mass was indeed Niagara, can hardly be called our first view of it. . . . It was a moonless night, and in the dusk we could only obscurely trace the vast vague outline of the two falls, divided by the blurred mass of shapeless shadows which we learned was Goat Island. As we looked upon them silently, and listened to the ceaseless boom like distant thunder, which shook the ground beneath our feet, across the snowy veil of the American Fall, to our left, shot rays of rosy light, which melted into amber, then into emerald. They were illuminating the great waters with colored calcium lights! * * But the brilliant rays which fell across the American Falls, and which were turned on and off like a dissolving view, did not reach to the Horse-Shoe Fall away to our right. Vast, solemn, shadowy, we could just distinguish its form in the darkness, could hear the deep murmur of its awful voice. And there, between it and us, what was *that* we saw? Was it some huge pale ghost standing sentinel before Niagara? White, spectral, motionless, it rose up and reached towards the stars—shapeless, dim, vague as a veiled ghost. There was something almost supernatural about it, it was like a colossal spectre, wrapped in a robe of strange dim light.

"'How fine and upright the column of spray is to-night,' said a strange voice beside us. This broke the illusion. But yet it seemed impossible that our ghost should be only a pillar of rising and falling spray! We saw it again, daily and nightly, but seldom again like that. We saw it blown along in clouds; we saw it like a great veil hiding the whole face of the Fall; we saw it one evening at sunset leaping and sparkling like a fountain of liquid gold,—but only once again did we see it rise up in that shape, the dim and ghostly guardian of the night.— *Through Cities and Prairie Lands.*

NIAGARA FALLS FROM CANADA.

TO GAZE into the face of the cataract and obtain a most comprehensive view of Niagara, one must stand upon the public road which follows the edge of the cliff on the Canada side. Approaching the Falls from the north, almost every step reveals new scenes and variations in a mighty and wondrous panorama. Here is the foot bridge, and within a few rods the road to the ferry winds its way to the water's edge below. The ferry boat, manned by veritable athletes, tosses like an egg-shell on the heaving and convulsed water, one moment gliding swiftly down the stream in the round of an eddy, the next, lifted up by a boiling wave as if it were tossed up from the scoop of a giant's hand beneath the water. Away southward "the cataract flashes, and thunders and agonizes—an almighty miracle of grandeur for ever going on;—the sight is riveted on the yeasty writhe in the abysm, and the solemn pillars of crystal eternally falling, like the fragments of some palace-crested star, descending through interminable space. The white field of the iris forms over the brow of the cataract, exhibits its radiant bow, and sails away in a vanishing cloud of vapor upon the wind; the tortured and convulsed surface of the caldron below shoots out its frothy and seething circles in perpetual torment; the thunders are heaped upon each other, the earth trembles;"—the rocks and woods around are tinged with the ever-changing rays of the rainbow; the spectator sees the whole sweep of the great cataract spread before him at once, in a fine panoramic view of both Falls. "Their general outline," from a description in Harper's Monthly, "bears a close resemblance to the shape of the human ear; the Horse-Shoe Fall constituting the upper lobe, while Goat Island and the American Fall represent the remaining portion. The river, whose general course has been east and west, makes a sharp turn to the right just at the point where the Fall now is. Its breadth is here contracted from three-fourths of a mile to less than one-fourth. The Horse-Shoe Fall only occupies the head of the chasm, while the American Cataract falls over its side; so that this Fall and a part of the Horse Shoe lie directly parallel with the Canada shore, and its whole extent can be taken in at a single glance. It is this oneness of aspect which renders the prospect from this side so much the more impressive for a first view of Niagara. It gives a strong, sharp outline which may afterward be filled up at leisure."

TABLE ROCK.

Within a short distance stands all that remains of the Table Rock; a narrow ledge along the bank, at the edge of the Horse-Shoe Fall. "On arriving at the great Horse-Shoe Fall," says Murray, "description must stop short; and to those who have not seen it, imagination must be left to finish a picture of which words can give but a feeble outline. How can language convey expressions too tremendous and sublime even for the mind to bear? How can it presume to embody a scene on which the eye could not gaze, to which the ear could not listen, and which the oppressed and overwhelmed power of reflection could not contemplate without feelings of awe, wonder, and delight, so intense as to amount almost to pain!"

> Who doth not feel, until his failing sight
> Faints into dimness with its own delight,
> His changing cheek, his sinking heart confess,
> The might —the majesty?
> — *Bride of Abydos.*

The sight is indeed impressive, the view entrancing, the abyss fascinating. Basil Hall mentions this curious effect: "It seemed to the imagination not impossible that the Fall might swell up and grasp us in its vortex. The actual presence of any very powerful moving object, is often more or less remotely connected with a feeling that its direction may be altered; and when the slightest variation would evidently prove fatal, a feeling of awe is easily excited. At all events, as I gazed upon the cataract, it more than once appeared to increase in its volume, and to be accelerated in its velocity, till my heated fancy became strained, alarmed, and so much overcrowded with new and old images,—all exaggerated,— that in spite of the conviction that the whole was nonsense, I felt obliged to draw back from the edge of the rock; and it required a little reflection and some resolution, to advance again to the brink." Guides and dresses can be procured at this point for a visit to the cavernous recess under the Great Fall.

GENERAL VIEW OF FALL FROM CANADA.

THE RAPIDS.

Apparently illimitable, seeming to pour from the blue sky, the Canadian Rapids are full before you. Forming a grand and striking feature in the scenery of Niagara, they are produced by the compression of the river to the width of two miles and a half just below the termination of Grand and Navy Islands; and by its course for the distance of three quarters of a mile over ledges of rugged rocks, making a descent of fifty-two feet on the American side, and fifty-seven on the Canada side. It is impossible to give an adequate idea of this rushing, boiling tide, that sweeps down, through the islands towards the verge, as if a myriad of war-steeds, neighing and panting, were contending with the most intense ferocity. The Rapids form the prelude to the grander displays of the Falls themselves, and viewed alone, are unequalled in their kind.

CLARK HILL ISLANDS.

On the road past Table Rock, and only a few rods distant, is Cedar Island, connected with the main land at either extremity by a pretty little truss bridge. On this island stands a Pagoda, over eighty feet in height, and a noticeable land-mark from all points in the vicinity of the Falls. Leaving Cedar Island, the Grand Rapids Drive is entered upon. It is one of the pleasantest roadways around Niagara, extending for a quarter of a mile close along the shore of the Canadian Rapids. The view it affords of the Rapids is grand, beyond description. Clark Hill Islands, five in number, situated in the rapids of the Niagara river, are connected, at either side, with the shore by an elegant suspension bridge of two hundred and fifty feet span. These two bridges have been appropriately named "Castor," and "Pollux." The scenery through the islands is of the most varied character; the quiet rippling of the narrow streams meandering among the well-wooded islands is in strong contrast to the turbulence of the waters that hurry on, washing the shores of the group. The whole scene is one of sweet repose.

THE BURNING SPRING.

At the eastern end of the bridge "Pollux," on the bank of the river, near the head of the Rapids, about a mile above the Falls, is located the Burning Spring. A gas flows through the water, which burns with a pale blue flame when ignited. It is described by the geologist Lyell, as follows: "Carburetted hydrogen, or, in the modern chemical phraseology, a light hydro-carbon, rises from beneath the water

ALONG THE BURNING SPRING DRIVE.

out of the limestone rock. The bituminous matter supplying this gas is probably of animal origin, as this limestone is full of marine mollusca, crustacea and corals, without vegetable remains, unless some fucoids may have decomposed in the same strata. The invisible gas makes its way in countless bubbles through the clear transparent waters of the Niagara. On the application of a lighted candle, it takes fire, and plays about with a lambent, flickering flame, which seldom touches the water, the gas being at first too pure to be inflammable, and only obtaining sufficient oxygen after mingling with the atmosphere." For the purpose of experiments, witnessed by the visitors, the gas is collected in a cylinder, allowed to pass out of the top of it through an inch pipe. After certain experiments are made, showing the tremendous force of the gas, the cylinder is removed, and the gas ignited on the surface of the water, through which it escapes.

ABOVE THE FALLS.

Following the old Portage road from the Burning Spring to the Falls, brings the

visitor to a point on the bluff, where the river makes a sharp, big inshore, along the tracks of the Michigan Central, and upon this spot a platform has been erected by the Company to allow undisturbed enjoyment of the most striking view of the Cataract. "Niagara should be first approached from above, and from the Canada shore," is a sentiment echoed and re-echoed by the writers of past generations: and the one comprehensive view, the grouping of Rapids and Islands and Falls and Gorge as seen from Falls View station on the Michigan Central Railroad, presents a picture of surpassing beauty. The vast concave of the Falls of Niagara opens upon your view. The American Fall forms the farther extremity of the semi-circle, breaking in a broad white sheet of foam upon a heap of rocks below. Close by its inner extremity is a gush of water —the Centre Fall—which in any other situation would be esteemed a considerable cascade, but here seems but a fragment of the larger cataract separated by a small rocky island in the bed of the river. The eye then rests upon the precipitous end of Goat Island, consisting of accumulated masses of stone, in horizontal strata, supporting a scanty covering of earth, and crowded to the edge with pines. Then the curve of the Horse-Shoe Fall rounds into prospect with full view of the Islands and the angry Canadian Rapids. "Your eye fixes upon some special white crest of

THE FIRST BRIDGE TO GOAT ISLAND ACROSS THE AMERICAN RAPIDS.

foam, and follows it down until it melts away into a smooth green surface rounding gently over, and disappearing in an abyss the depth of which you cannot see. This green slope sweeps round in a magnificent curve to the right; beyond this is a purple-gray precipice, and still further on a white cataract flashing back the sunbeams. From the centre of the curve, a pillar of spray floats calmly up, with the crown of a rainbow just rising above the verge of the abyss." And again, and again, will the eye wander from right to left, and from left to right; from the point of the American Fall to the near shore line of the Horse-Shoe, and vice-versa, sweeping around the circumference of the majestic curve of Niagara. At a short distance from this point a very pretty glimpse of the American Fall can be caught through an opening in the bank designated as the "Jolly Cut."

LUNDY'S LANE.

To the west, about one and one-half miles distant, stands a tower erected upon the famous battle-field of Lundy's Lane. On July 25th, 1814, the decisive battle of the war was fought here. An old campaigner who does the honors at the observatory (and though old campaigners live and die, the one occupying the post, is an original old campaigner, *spiritually* to say the least,)— has, they say, two versions of the action, which he produces as he supposes may suit the nationality  of his auditors. The story goes, however, that years ago, General Scott was regaled with the English version, and then learned for the first time how thoroughly he was beaten upon that well-contested field. Through the village of Drummondville, the original Canadian city at the Falls, so called in honor of General Drummond, the traveler wends his way along a pleasant road to the

WHIRLPOOL RAPIDS

just below the old Suspension Bridge. Here a staircase and also an inclined railway conducts one easily and safely to the platform below, whence the sight of the old bridge above, the roaring rapids, the distant whirlpool, and the shady walk along the water's edge, give splendid views. The whole volume of water rushes by with marvelous rapidity, boiling and seething in its narrow channels.

THE WHIRLPOOL.

Below the Whirlpool Rapids is situated one of the most remarkable features of the gorge of Niagara—the Whirlpool,—worthy of more attention than is usually given to it by visitors in general. Brock's Monument, erected on the Queenston Heights, four miles distant, is visible from this point, and the Niagara river winds away to the north, till it is lost in Lake Ontario beyond.

THE ROAR OF THE FALLS.

RESPECTING the thundering of the waters, the eternal roar of the cataract, many and conflicting are the statements handed down to us by the writers of two centuries past. Father Hennepin, in a most candid manner, states its deafening powers, and in his sketch, represents the members of the observation party holding their hands to the ears, to shut out, as it were, the unpleasant and terrific sounds. Robert Sutcliff, in 1805, writes: "I could very distinctly hear the noise of the Falls of Niagara, although then about twenty-four miles from that stupendous cataract. The distance at which the people in these parts say the Falls may be heard, when the wind and other concurrent circumstances are favorable, is almost incredible. I met with a reputable looking farmer, driving a team of four fine oxen upon the road, who told me, with all the gravity of a man speaking the truth, that he sometimes heard them very plainly at his residence, forty miles distant, when the air was calm and serene."

Duncan, in 1818, says: "Most of the accounts of the Falls mention that the sound of them is heard at a very great distance. This is comparatively seldom the case. I have been told, in the neighborhood, that in particular states of the barometer, and especially before stormy weather, the sound of the cataract is heard twenty miles off, or even farther; but on several occasions I could with difficulty distinguish it at a distance of two miles, and sometimes, I understand, it does not reach so far."

Ten years later, in 1828, Stuart states positively: "We distinctly heard the sound of the cataract, about ten miles from the Falls; but it is often heard at a far greater distance in favorable states of the wind and atmosphere."

Charles Dickens, the great English novelist, in *American Notes*, gives his experience as follows: "I am inclined to think that the noise of the Falls is very much exaggerated; and this will appear the more probable when the depth of the great basin in which the water is received is taken into account. At no time during our stay there was the wind at all high or boisterous, but we never heard them three miles off, even at the very quiet time of sunset, though we often tried."

Some assert that along the course of the river, the sound is perceptible at a distance of fourteen miles. Yet it is scarcely heard within the precincts of the Falls, above and at a little distance from them. Indeed, the wonder is to the visitor, not that the cadence is so great, but so small, compared with the quantity of water that falls and the immense height from which it is precipitated.

DEPTHS OF NIAGARA'S CANYON.

W. H. BALLOU.

MANY ATTEMPTS were made previous to the government survey in 1876, to obtain the depth of the water in the canyon below the Falls. Bars of railroad iron, pails of stones, and all unreasonable and awkward instruments were attached to long lines and lowered from the railway suspension bridge, but positively refused to sink. The reason for this is obvious. The very bulk of the instruments was sufficient, no matter what their weight, to give the powerful undercurrent the means to buoy them upon or near the surface. Our party, however, with a small sounding lead of twelve pounds weight, attached to a slender cord, easily obtained the depths from the Falls to the railway suspension bridge. One day we launched a small boat at the inclined railway, and entered on a most exciting and perilous exploration of this part of the canyon. The old guide, long in charge of the miniature ferry situated here, accompanied the party. With great difficulty we approached within a short distance of the American Falls, which darted great jets of water upon us and far out into the stream. The roar was so terrible that no voice or human sound, however near we were to one another, could be heard. The leadsman cast the line, which passed rapidly down, and told of eighty-three feet. This was quite near the shore. Passing out of the friendly eddy which had assisted us so near the Falls we shot rapidly down the stream. The next cast of the lead read one hundred feet, deepening to one hundred and ninety-three feet at the inclined railway. The average depth to the Swift Drift, where the river suddenly becomes narrow, with a velocity too great to be measured, was one hundred and fifty-three feet. Just under the railway bridge the whirlpool rapids set in, and so violently are the waters agitated that they rise like ocean billows to the height of twenty feet. At this point I computed the depth at two hundred and ten feet, which was accepted as approximately correct.

The geological formation of Niagara's canyon is too well understood to bear comment. Some of the topographical appearances, however, may be mentioned. The canyon's walls range from two hundred and seventy to three hundred and sixty feet in height above the water level. Of course, they are highest at their termination at Lewiston, where, on the opposite side, the base of Brock's Monument is three hundred and sixty-five feet above water in the canyon. The walls are continually crumbling owing to the action of the atmosphere, frost and miniature springs. The *débris* is driven out into Lake Ontario, forming what are known as the Brickbat Shoals, situated three and a half miles from the river's mouth. The river within the walls, more especially where the canyon is narrow, is subject to rise and fall at short intervals, if the wind is heavy on Lake Erie.

AMERICAN FALLS FROM GOAT ISLAND.

IN WINTER.

VERY FEW persons, comparatively, are aware of the scenes of surpassing beauty presented by the Cataract of Niagara, in winter. Its appearance is then much more attractive and glorious, than in the summer.

The trees are covered with the most brilliant and sparkling coruscations of snow and ice; the islands, the shrubs, the giant rocks, are robed in the same spotless vesture. Frozen spray, glittering and gleaming as brightly and vivaciously as frozen sunlight, encases all things; Niagara Falls is the absolute dominion of the Ice King. In bright sunshine, the flashing rays from millions of gems produce a bewitching effect. "At such a moment the characteristic attributes of Niagara seem fused and heightened into 'something more exquisite still.' Its intrinsic sublimity and beauty experience a liberal transfiguration. Nature is visibly idealized. Nothing more brilliant or enchanting can be conceived. The brightest tales of magic 'pale their ineffectual fires.' Islands, whose flowers are thickset diamonds, and forests, whose branches are glittering with brilliants, and amethysts, and pearls, seem no longer a luxurious figment of genius, but a living and beaming reality. One feels in the midst of such blazing coruscations and such glorious bursts of radiance, as if the magician's ring had been slipped upon his finger unawares, and, rubbed unwittingly, had summoned the gorgeous scene before him. It is as if Mammoth Cave, with its groves of stalactites, and crystal bowers, and gothic avenues and halls, and star chambers, and flashing grottoes, were suddenly uncapped to the wintery sun, and bathed in his thrilling beams; or as if the fabled palace of Neptune had risen abruptly from the deep, and were flinging its splendors in the eye of heaven."

Upon the occurrence of a thaw sufficient to break up the ice in Lake Erie, masses of floating ice, dissevered from the frozen lake and stream above, are precipitated over the Falls in blocks of several tons each. These remain at the foot of the cataract, from the stream being closed below, "and form a natural bridge across it. As they accumulate, they get progressively piled up, like a Cyclopean wall, built of huge blocks of ice instead of stone. This singular masonry of nature gets cemented by the spray,

BEHIND THE HORSE-SHOE FALL IN WINTER—"ICY FOLIAGE AND FORMS."

which rising in clouds of mist as usual from the foot of the Falls, attaches itself in its upward progress to the icy wall, and soon gets frozen with the rest of the mass, helping to fill up the interstices between the larger blocks of which this architecture is composed."

This icy wall or mound rises up from the base of the torrent in a bulwark of pyramidal form, in front of the Falls, within a few feet of the edge of the precipice, to a height of from twenty to forty feet above the level of the upper stream. Scaling the mound is an exhilarating and laborious exercise, but the near sight of the maddened waters plunging into the depths of an unfathomable vortex below, is a fitting reward for the adventurous undertaking.

The ice-bridge generally extends from the Horse-Shoe Fall, to a point near the Railway bridge, lasts generally from two to three months, and is crossed by hundreds of foot passengers during the winter. The ice forming the bridge is ordinarily from one hundred to one hundred and fifty feet thick—rising from fifty to sixty feet above the natural surface of the river. The tinge of the waters, from the dark green of summer, is changed to a muddy yellow; huge icicles, formed by an accumulation of frozen spray, hang perpendicularly from the rocks; the trees on Goat Island and Prospect Park seem partially buried; a mass of quaint and curious crystalline forms stand in lieu of the bushes; the buildings seem to sink under ponderous coverings of snow and ice; the tops of trees and points of rock on which the dazzling white frost work does not lie, stand out in bold contrast, forming the deep shadows of the entrancing picture; the whole presents a wild, savage aspect, grand and imposing.

Goat Island remains, in winter, one of the chief centers of attraction. A prominent English physician, Dr. Wm. Sharp, writes: "I can never forget my first visit to it in December, 1880. The snow was falling thickly at the time. Old Nicholson constituted himself as guide and proved to be both useful and amusing. The Canadian side was altogether hidden by the hazy mist of the falling snow, and never since or before did I look upon a scene so awfully grand and impressive as Niagara then presented. There, with old Nicholson in the back ground, I was alone with nature. A sense of vague immensity that was almost appalling engrossed the attention. All was solitude, vastness and silence, save the deep thunder of the Falls that swelled ever like a mighty anthem, and as if in keeping with the weird sublimity of the scene, two gulls, like restless, wandering spirits of the deep, swept ceaselessly to and fro, now vanishing from sight and now emerging from the mist and gloom."

If one can see Niagara but once, it had better be in winter than in summer. The scene is one of peerless grandeur, worth going hundreds of miles to behold.

A BOLD SWIM.

Captain Webb's Foolhardy Feat.

RASH IS THE man who incurs risk or hazard from a mere impulse without counting the cost; adventurous is he who does it from a love of the arduous and the bold; foolhardy he who throws himself into danger in disregard or defiance of the consequences. These qualifications of the mad attempt made by Captain Matthew Webb to swim down the Whirlpool Rapids and through the Whirlpool, on the 24th day of July, 1883, are certainly, in view of the facts, not too severe strictures. Moved by a desire for notoriety, this bold and brave athlete, who had many times faced the surging billows of an angry sea, without other means of safety than nature had provided him, announced his purpose to swim the Whirlpool Rapids in the Niagara River. This was heralded by the press, and discussions as to the possibilities and chances of success agitated many minds. Captain Webb looked upon the scheme as a pleasant undertaking. His friends and the public looked upon it as certain death. The great swimmer was confident that he could make the trip in safety. He carefully looked over the ground, but he had failed to realize the immensity of the undertaking, and so deliberately gave up his life.

Captain Webb was a native of Shropshire, England, and the son of a physician. He went to sea at an early age, and became the captain of a merchantman. He first attracted public notice by jumping from the Cunard mail steamer "Russia," during a storm, to save a sailor who fell overboard. For this he received at the hands of the Duke of Edinburgh the first gold medal given by the Royal Humane Society. In 1875 he accomplished his greatest feat, swimming across the English Channel from Dover to Calais. The trial took place August 24th and 25th, and after a desperate struggle with the choppy sea he accomplished the distance of twenty-five miles in 21h. 45min., the best time on record. He has visited this country several times. On August 13th, 1879, he swam from Sandy Hook to Manhattan Beach, Coney Island, a distance in line of ten miles. Owing to the tides and the fact that his contract would not permit him to land at the island before five P. M., he was in the water eight hours and swam in all about sixteen miles. He was a man of powerful physique, being six feet one inch tall, finely proportioned and weighing about two hundred pounds in condition. He was forty years of age. He leaves a wife and two children. He has accumulated $15,000 by his exhibitions.

For three-quarters of a mile below the Suspension Bridge run the Whirlpool Rapids, the wildest and most tumultuous portion of the river Niagara. The tremendous power of the current cannot be realized. The whole force of the water concentrates itself here; it seems as though it would tear asunder the steep, wooded hills that enclose it, so the river, where the wild and startling is its water, ceaselessly terrific power. As far coming down from as the eye can reach the Falls in immense the waters thunder volume, is compressed down in seething, heav- into a space much too ing masses, lashed into small for it, and meet- foam, dashing and ing with this resist- whirling into angry ance, gathers its billows twenty or mighty force in one su- thirty feet high, preme effort, and through the narrow mounting higher and passes of the gorge, higher, dashes past the until it reaches its bend in one continuous climax at the bend in but changing surge of water, resembling nothing so much as the roll of the ocean on a lea shore. One hundred million tons of water passing over the Falls' cliff every hour, crowd through this narrow defile, less than three hundred feet in width, thundering along at a velocity of twenty-seven miles an hour. At no other point does the terrific force of Niagara so create wonderfully realistic impressions upon the beholder.

> ERE THE long valley crooks, and the flight of the river is broken;
> Headlong it plunges, despairing, and beats on the bars of its prison;
> Beats, and runs wildly from wall to wall, then strives to recover,
> Beats on another still, and around the circle is carried,
> Jostled from shoulder to shoulder, till losing its galloping motion,
> Dizzily round it swirls, and is dragged toward the hideous Whirlpool.
>
> Round sweeps the horrible maelstrom, and into the whirl of its vortex
> Circle a broken boat, an oar-blade, things without number;
> Striving, they shove one another, and seem to hurry, impatient
> To measure the shadowy will-be, and seek from their torment a respite.
>
> Legs that have leapt the Falls and swum unseen 'neath the current,
> Here are restored again, and weird is their resurrection;
> Here like straws they are snapt, and grinding like millstones together,
> Chafing and splintering their mates, they wade in their deepening ruins;
>
> Till, without hope, on tiptoe they rise, lips shriveled and speechless,
> Seeing sure fate before them that tightens its toils to ensnare them;
> Hollow the hell-hole gapes, and ravenously it receives them,—
> All that is left is a sigh, and the echoes of that are soon strangled.
>   —*Houghton's Niagara.*

Such was the course selected by the plucky and resolute sailor for his exhibition of power and endurance—through a fearful channel, an eternal war of waters. From a boat rowed to the center of the stream, at a point about one-quarter mile from the head of the rapids, Captain Webb dived head first into the water. It was just twenty minutes past four o'clock. A few vigorous strokes and he was fairly in the rapids, going breast on, his form a mere speck, as seen from the great bluff above. He went like an arrow shot from a bow. The first great wave he struck he went under, but in a second appeared way beyond. The great waves seethed over him occasionally, but he always seemed ready to meet them. His great chest was boldly pushed forward, and occasionally half of the magnificent physique of the reckless adventurer was lifted from the water, but he bravely kept his position through it all and seemed perfectly collected and at home. So the mad journey went on safely through the upper rapids. He passed then through the lower ones. There the waves dash higher, up one of his arms, as the water is confined in if to signal some unforeseen danger. A second a narrower space, and later he was buried in the trip is in every way more perilous. How far the foaming billows, he went alive no one which dash upwards will ever know. He was forty or fifty feet, and seen by many while whirl and seethe as if passing through this lashed by a thousand awful sea. His body furies. This was the was borne onward, now last seen of the intrepid rising above, now sinking swimmer,—his disappearance occurring thirteen minutes after he capped waves. He was seen to enter the whirlpool. Here he threw active search was insti-

tuted but no trace of his body had been found when the shades of night enveloped the troubled waters in a mantle of darkness.

During the afternoon of July 28th, the body was recovered in the river below Lewiston. The arms were extended as though in the act of taking a swimming stroke, and the feet were likewise extended as though in the act of swimming. The scalp had a deep gash about four inches long, and the hips and left shoulder had long blue marks where the body had struck the rocks.

Theories as to the direct cause of death are rife. Was the life crushed out of him by the weight of the water; was he drowned; or did he loose his life by diving and striking on a jagged stone or rock? These are questions surrounded with inscrutable mystery.

The official report, of the medical examiners, at the inquest held over the noted swimmer's remains, states that no bones were found broken, and the wounds were none of them sufficient to have caused death. The muscular tissue was peculiar; when the scalpel was used shreds of desiccated muscle would be carried along and collect on the edge of the knife. The blood was very red, showing that it had not been deoxidized by asphyxia. "As the result of our examination," say the examiners, "we are led to the conclusion that death was caused not by asphyxia or drowning, or by any local injury by the body coming in contact with any hard substance, but by the shock from the reactionary force of the water in the rapids coming in contact with the submerged body with sufficient force to instantly destroy the respiratory power, and in fact all vital action, by direct pressure and force of contact—a shock of sufficient intensity to paralyze the nerve centres, partially desiccate the muscular tissues, and forestall any possible sequel of death by drowning. The cause of death in passing through the rapids being thus constant and in no way accidental, as might be the case in drowning, forces the conclusion that no living body can pass through the rapids alive. In the first breaker he was submerged and subjected to this pressure, death resulting."

This strongly sustains the first theory, and the appearance of the blood dispels entirely the second one, that of drowning. As to the third, its supporters claim undisputable evidence in the disclosure of a new fact. It has been generally conceded that the water from the Falls to the Whirlpool was very deep, and that no rocks were within many feet of the surface. This is contradicted by George Barker, who for twenty years has been taking views of the river and of the Falls. He says: "One morning a few years ago I visited the Whirlpool Rapids for the purpose of taking some instantaneous photographs. The water was very low, caused by a heavy wind which had been blowing up the river above the Falls for several days. I was surprised to find that the points where usually were to be seen immense splashes, which are the great attractions of the Whirlpool Rapids, rocks were plainly to be seen, at some points just at the surface, at others rising out of the water two or three feet. Several negatives taken at the time, show immense rocks lying right in the course which Webb took in his fatal attempt. The views show beyond a doubt that the rapids of the Niagara river are studded with rocks, and the post mortem examiners may be wrong in their conclusions."

This attempt of Captain Webb, although a failure, has brought to the front, numerous bold adventurers with unheard of schemes, such as descend the Falls, scale the mountains of falling waters, dive into the Whirlpool, walk across the upper rapids, etc., which, if carried into effect, will add new zest and spice to the ancient chronicles of Niagara's accidents and incidents, so diversely and wondrously elaborated by the loquacious hackman-guide of the Falls.

PILGRIMAGE UNDER THE FALLS

INTERNATIONAL PARK PROJECT.

IN THE fall of 1878, Lord Dufferin, then Governor-General of Canada, suggested the idea of creating an International Park at Niagara, from lands adjacent to and including the Falls, to be taken from both sides of the river. Governor Robinson, of New York, was cordially in favor of the project, and the New York Legislature appointed a commission to investigate the subject and report thereon. In 1879, Mr. James T. Gardner, director of the New York State Survey, and Mr. Frederick Law Olmsted reported to the Legislature. The Canadian Government had also a survey made, embracing all the lands between the embankment above and the river front, and has been ready at all times to co-operate with the State of New York.

The press and the pulpit took up the agitation of the question. Rev. Robert Collyer at the Church of the Messiah in New York made it the subject of an elaborate discourse. After extolling the glories of the place, he catalogued, in a forcible manner, the shames of Niagara, in substance as follows: "One of the greatest shames was cutting down a long, sweeping arbor, through which in such grand beauty the Falls used to loom up to view half a mile away, and through which the deep, soft thunders of the mighty cataract fell upon the ear, a grand diapason. The whole surroundings were now changed. There was not a touch of sacredness. Mammon ruled. Of course those owning the land had a right to use it as they thought best. It was, however, clearly the duty of the sovereign people of the State of New York to purchase it. This thing had gone far enough. The noble park should be kept free to all visitors, the waters should be rescued from the hordes of mills, and all the land about the grand water flood be given to the world free."

This matter of an International Park lingered, however, till this summer, when a commission empowered by the New York Legislature, to select and locate the lands most desirable for the object in view, and institute proceedings for acquiring the title to these lands, met at Niagara Falls. The result of their deliberations is briefly told by ex-Lieut.-Gov. Dorsheimer, the president of the commission: "At the conclusion of our inspection we determined to take all of the islands in the river within the jurisdiction of this State, both Goat, Bird, Luna, Chapin, and a few more adjacent to Niagara river. In addition to the islands we selected a strip of land on the main shore, beginning just above the head of the rapids, and ending at the upper suspension bridge." The selection embraces the lands immediately around the Falls, and the possession of this territory by the State of New York would prove sufficient for the preservation of the scenery. It is the opinion of many that the Whirlpool Rapids and Whirlpool are the natural complement of the Falls, and should by all means be included in the proposed park. Whatever may be the decision arrived at upon this last point, a Niagara Reservation may now be considered as a settled fact.

A PLEA FOR PRESERVATION.

RECOGNIZING as I do the unspoiled value of Niagara as a source or means of strength, refreshment, and happiness for many millions of men and women, and of elevation and beauty in our National character, and feeling most deeply interested in the effort to restore and preserve it for these high uses, I am of the opinion that if the ground about the Fall were really needed for cotton and paper mills, or any other necessary and productive human industries, it would be right to take it and appropriate and occupy it for these objects. We shall have a vast and crowded population in this part of our country before any great time has elapsed, and we are preparing conditions here in America under which the mass of men must, in large degree, live for bread for themselves, and little beyond. Whenever there is a real conflict or antagonism between economic, business or industrial interests on the one hand, and ideal or æsthetic considerations on the other, the latter must give way, and rightly, because they are secondary or subordinate when compared with the necessities of physical subsistence. But in this case of Niagara Falls, and the question of its preservation or destruction, there is no good reason for "huddling factories around the Falls,"— no need of it whatever. I think it the idlest thing in the world for anybody who desires the preservation of the scenery here for ideal and spiritual uses to decry or contemn the commercial spirit or business energy of our time, or to lament its application to this particular object,— the utilization of the waterpower of Niagara for manufacturing purposes. He is a poor, shallow poet or artist who can see only the poetic or artistic side of things. The mass of men must always toil. Infinite drudgery is required to sustain human life under the conditions of civilized society. Millions of men must labor — must labor honestly, nobly, and happily — that one great poet may sing their life, or one man of divine genius paint a picture of immortal power and beauty.

Build the factories, then, and let Niagara turn their wheels. But where shall the factories stand? It would be a most insane and outrageous thing to place them here, amid these scenes unparalleled on the planet. It would be a wholly wanton sacrilege, a profanation unusually culpable, because entirely unnecessary. The

Niagara River above the Falls lies so high above all the country below them that the water can be taken almost anywhere from the river channel. Only a very small region immediately adjacent to the cataract and the rapids, with the islands in the river—this is all that is required to make this place, or keep it what nature made it, a place endowed, as no other place on the globe is endowed, with qualities suited to refresh, elevate, and gladden the mind and heart of civilized man forever. It is a sad error and wrong that this small territory, which includes all that is essential to Niagara,—all its wild grace and ineffable charm,—should be held by any private or individual ownership. It should be the property of the State, the possession of the people, and should be held in trust and cared for by the government. All its wealth of beauty and of high uses should be accessible to the poorest children of toil who may, by wise forethought or self-denying frugality, save from the price of their labor the means for a pilgrimage to this shrine of ideal and spiritual reality.

For we must have something besides factories, and turbine wheels, and supply and demand, and daily toil for daily bread, even for the toiler himself, so that he may have "a daily beauty in his life," to use Shakespeare's phrase. You see, gentlemen capitalists and manufacturers, the laborer must toil *happily*, or you may all come to grief together, and capital must supply and maintain the conditions of beauty and happiness for him. Labor, directed and ennobled by the ideal, moral or spiritual element, creates everything; but a democratic civilization, based on the labor of a class of serfs of the mine and mill, whose toil is unwilling, degraded, and faithless, would not be likely to endure long in a world where the deepest meaning of everything is moral.

Let us have a great city of factories, sustained by the water-power of Niagara. We are destined to have it. It is entirely right that this immense endowment of mechanical forces for the use of mankind should be employed to supply their physical wants. Only let us have the mills a little at one side; not just here at the Falls. There are quite as good and even better sites for them a little farther away. Put them far enough back from the Falls and the Rapids to give room for a screen of trees between,—far enough for the distance to soften the clangor of steam whistles, so that on Sunday, or (as I observe that many laborers in New England mills have to work on Sunday) at least on the Fourth of July, the toiler of the factory may come to the Falls, and, looking upon their grandeur and noble purity, undefiled by tawdry electric lights, or watching the wild play of the rapids, or wandering amid the solitudes of "the forest primeval" on Goat Island, may feel that he has a soul, and is not a mere driven beast of burden, and that he has a country which cares for him as one of the great brotherhood of her children.—*Boston Advertiser.*

THE NEW CANTILEVER BRIDGE ACROSS NIAGARA RIVER.

ACROSS NIAGARA RIVER.

The New Michigan Central Bridge.

A VERITABLE marvel of engineering, the canti-lever bridge uniting Canada and the United States, over the rushing torrent of the Niagara, at an altitude of two hundred and thirty-nine ft., is one among the attractive monuments evidencing the spirit of our progressive age, and the advance made in recent years in the art of bridge-building. In less than eight months, from the time of beginning operations, this elegant structure has been reared—perfect in every detail, substantial, safe and firm as the Rock of Ages!

The location of the bridge, a short distance below the Falls of Niagara, precluding the possibility of any supports in the center of the stream, which at this point is 500 feet from shore to shore at the water's edge; and the construction of a suspension bridge being unadvisable on account of the very great expense and interminable time involved, and also the inevitable wave-motion of that class of structures when loads are moved over them, necessitated a peculiar manner of construction, and a style different from that of any bridge already constructed.

The design is what is known as the canti-lever bridge, the principle of which is that of a trussed beam, supported at or near its centre, with the arms extending each way, and one end anchored or counterweighed to provide for unequal loading. It is in practice an entirely new design, no other bridge as yet having been completed upon this principle.

Each end is made up of a section, entirely of steel, extending from the shore nearly half way over the chasm. Each section is supported near its center by a strong steel tower, from which extend two lever arms, one reaching the rocky bluffs, the other extending over the river 175 feet beyond the towers. The outer arm having no support, and being subject like the other to the weight of trains, a counter advantage is given by the shore arm being firmly anchored to the rocks on the shore. The towers on either side rise from the water's edge; between them a clear span of 495 feet over the river, the longest double-track truss span in the world. The ends of the canti-levers reaching on each side 395 feet from the abutments, leave a gap of 120 feet filled by an ordinary truss bridge hung from the ends of the canti-levers. Here provision is made for expansion and contraction by an ingenious arrangement between the ends of the truss bridge and of the canti-levers allowing the ends to move freely as the temperature changes, but at the same time preserving perfect rigidity against side pressure from the wind. There are no guys for this purpose, as in a suspension bridge, but the structure is complete within itself. The total length of the bridge is 910 feet. It has a double track and is built strong enough to carry upon each track at the same time a freight train of the heaviest kind extending the entire length of the bridge, headed by two "consolidation" engines, and under a side pressure of thirty pounds per square foot, which pressure is produced by a wind having a velocity of seventy-five miles per hour, and even then will be strained to only one-fifth of its ultimate strength.

The foundations rest on the solid rock; four blocks of most substantial masonry are carried up fifty feet above the surface of the water and from these the steel towers supporting the canti-levers rise 130 feet. The load of 1,600 tons that come upon each pair of steel columns is so distributed that the pressure upon the foundation rocks is only 25 pounds per square inch. From the tower foundations up, the whole bridge is steel, every inch of which was subjected to the most rigid tests from the time it left the ore to the time it entered the structure.

The structure has very much the appearance of an ordinary truss bridge, but, in view of the conditions and surroundings, very different in the manner of its erection. The towers on the water's edge and the shore arms of the canti-levers have, of course, been erected with the help of temporary scaffoldings and a resting point on *terra-firma* and the superstructure is easily put in place from the shore to the steel towers. But after this comes the difficult portion of the work, i. e., to span the 495 feet across and 239 feet above a roaring river whose force no earthly power can stay. No temporary structure could survive a moment, and here the skill of the engineer came in to baffle nature and laugh at her powers. The design of the canti-lever is such that after the shore arm is completed and anchored, the river arm is built out, one panel or section at a time by means of great traveling derricks, and self-sustaining as it progresses. After one panel of twenty-five feet is built and has its bracing adjusted, the traveling derrick is moved forward and another panel erected. Thus the work progresses, section by section, until the ends of the canti-lever are reached, when a truss bridge is swung across the gap of 120 feet, resting on the ends of the canti-lever arms, thus forming the connecting link. This great work will remain for ages a fitting tribute to the earnestness, enterprise and energy of the Michigan Central management, and its successful completion in so short a time reflects great credit upon the advancement of American engineering and the ability and skill of the contractors the Central Bridge Works, of Buffalo, N. Y.

PROGRESS OF THE WORK.

WORK on foundations began April 15th, and the introduction of the "beton coignet" began June 6th and was completed June 20 on the American side, and seven days later on the Canada side. The first stone for the piers on the American side was laid June 26, and on the Canada side July 13. The American piers were capped August 20, and the Canadian September 3. On August 29 the first column of steel for the tower was lowered on the American side, and on the Canada side September 10. The last section of the American tower had been laid two days previous, and on the Canadian tower it was put down September 18. On the 24th the first iron for the cantilever was run out and both cantilevers were completed on the 17th of November. Temporary scaffoldings of timber were built from the bluff on either side out to the edge of the water on a level with the top of the tower. Upon these the shore-arms of the canti levers were erected, one end resting on the steel towers and the other upon masonry on the bluff. The shore end was firmly anchored to this masonry, so that it will take an uplifting force of 1000 tons at each end to displace it. This constitutes the counter-weight to balance the unequal loading on the river arm. As this, under the most unfavorable conditions, can never exceed 340 tons, the provision is ample.

There will not be any of that wave motion noticed on a suspension bridge as a train moves over it. Remembering that it took over three years to build the present suspension bridge for a single track, that this bridge for a double track, not only had to be finished within seven and a half months from the execution of the contract, but has been actually completed with eight days to spare, it reflects great credit upon the advancement of American engineering skill, as exemplified by the ability, capacity and skill of all who have been associated with the project in positions of responsibility. 400,000 feet of timber and fifteen tons of bolts were consumed in the false work. The piers contain 1,100 cubic yards of "beton coignet," and the abutments of the approaches 1,000 cubic yards of masonry. The traveling derricks are the largest yet built. They are calculated to sustain a weight of thirty-two tons on the overhanging arm, and project forty feet beyond any support. It is the only bridge of any magnitude completed upon this principle. The Firth of Forth bridge in Scotland, with a clear span of 1,600 feet, is to be built upon this plan, and also in this country the Fraser River bridge, 315 feet clear span, on the Canadian Pacific. These are the only examples of this design yet undertaken, but the principle especially recommends itself to long span bridges that must be erected without false work.

The total weight of the iron and steel entering into the composition of this massive structure is about 3,000 tons. The excavations were carried down until solid rock was reached, when blocks of "beton coignet" twenty feet wide and

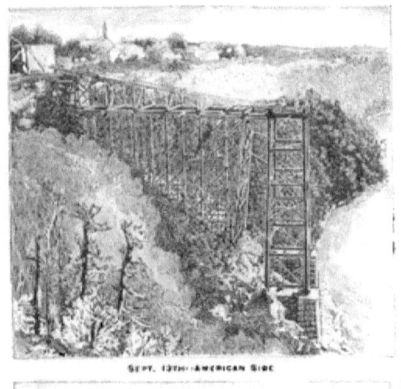
SEPT. 13TH—AMERICAN SIDE.

SEPT. 15TH—CANADA SIDE.

OCT. 30—CANADA SIDE.

NOV. 4TH—AMERICAN SIDE.

NOV. 14TH—AMERICAN SIDE.

NOV. 12TH—CANADA SIDE.

CANTILEVER BRIDGE AT VARIOUS STAGES OF CONSTRUCTION.

forty-five feet long and ten feet thick were put in. These form one single mass capable of withstanding a pressure almost equal to the best Quincy granite, interlocking with the boulders in sides and bottom of pit, and so distributes the load of 1,600 tons that comes upon each pair of steel columns as to produce a pressure on the natural formation much less than a fashionable young lady brings upon the heel of her French boot every time she steps. The total weight resting on each of the towers under a maximum condition of strain is in round numbers 3,200 tons. Each ingot of steel was submitted to a chemical analysis, and samples to a mechanical test. The standard of excellence adopted was more severe and exacting than usual, and all steel that failed to meet the requirements was rejected.

The superstructure was designed by engineers Schneider and Hayes. General Field gave his personal attention for over seven months to all of the many questions connected with the building of such an important structure, and the entire field work has been under his directions. His plans have been ably carried out by superintendent of erection, S. V. Ryland, assisted by foreman A. Deyo, W. A. Lee and Thos. J. Sullivan. The shop organization of the Central Bridge Works, Mr. R. D. Wilson, Supt., is also entitled to much credit. The force consists of about 160 men all of whom have seemed to take a personal interest in the great work. Mr. Schneider's staff consisted of A. R. True, principal assistant, and J. A. Bell and B. F. Betts, assistant engineers, W. F. Zimmermann, inspector of material at the mills, and J. Jung, shop inspector.

On the morning of November 21, 1883, the work of putting in the fixed span began, and when the hour of noon had arrived the sections had been connected, and the bridge practically completed. The weather during this performance was very bad, but a large crowd of spectators, which included ladies, railroad officials and bridge experts, stood patiently in the midst of a heavy rain storm and interestedly watched the operation.

In the afternoon of November 21, the Central Bridge Works closed their shops and the entire force, under charge of Supt. Wilson, visited the bridge, their employers furnishing free transportation.

The capacity of their works and the ability and strength of their organization, needs no better monument than the cantilever bridge they have just completed, which, for novelty and excellence of design, and unprecedented time within which a work of this magnitude has been brought to successful completion, has not its equal in the history of engineering science.

December 20th, 1883, a scientific test, under direction of prominent engineers took place in the presence of a vast concourse of spectators from all sections of the United States. The structure was pronounced safe as the safest, substantial, enduring and firm, a real triumph of engineering skill, management and enterprise.

AN OLD HUNTER

OFFENBACH ON NIAGARA.

From Notes of a Travelling Musician.

MUCH has been written on the subject of this wonderful waterfall, but no one has yet been able to describe the impression produced by the sight of the great stream at the moment when it leaps headlong, from a height of a hundred and fifty feet, into the fathomless abyss beneath. The view of that vast amphitheatre, of that prodigious volume of water, breaking into foam, with a roar of thunder, like the huge tidal wave that follows an earthquake, made me giddy, and caused me to forget all I had ever read, all I had ever heard, and all that had ever suggested itself to my imagination. This diluvial torrent, framed within the wildest scenery, surrounded by lofty trees of the deepest green, upon which a shower of spray is constantly falling like perpetual dew, defies photography, painting, or description. In order to describe, there must be some point of comparison. To what can Niagara be compared, that unrivalled, everlasting phenomenon, to the magnificence of which we can never become accustomed!

While we were absorbed in the contemplation of this wonder —

"This is the spot," said our guide, "where an Indian met with his fate a fortnight ago. Carried away by the current, the slight craft that held him was drawing near to the Falls, notwithstanding all his efforts. The Indian, feeling his strength giving way, saw that he was lost. He ceased to struggle, wrapped himself up in his red blanket as in a shroud, and laid himself down in the bottom of his boat. A few seconds after he was on the crest of the gigantic wave, and was shot with the rapidity of lightning into this watery grave, covered with a mist of immaculate white."

After hearing the story of this catastrophe, so fearful, yet so grand, I could not help envying the fate of the unfortunate red-skin, and I wondered that all Americans in distress did not prefer the Falls of Niagara to the insipid revolver. After having long enjoyed this wonderful spectacle, I crossed the bridge and set foot on Canadian soil. Here, I had been told, I would see Indians. I expected to find savages, and was surprised to find only dealers in bric-à-brac. They were hideous, I confess; they looked quite ferocious, I admit also; but I doubt whether they were genuine Indians. However that may be, they surrounded me on all sides, offered me bamboos, fans, cigar-holders, and pocket-books of a doubtful taste. They reminded me of the Indians of the forest of Fontainebleau who sell pen-holders and paper-knives.

Nevertheless, I made a few purchases; but I verily believe that I brought back into France some curiosities which had been procured at the selling out of some Parisian bazar.

SPECULATIONS OF THE SCIENTISTS.

RETROCESSION OF THE FALLS.

SIR CHARLES LYELL.

WE FIRST came in sight of the Falls of Niagara when they were about three miles distant. The sun was shining full upon them—no building in view—nothing but the green wood, the falling water and the white foam. At that moment they appeared to me more beautiful than I had expected, and less grand; but after several days, when I had enjoyed a nearer view of the two cataracts, had listened to their thundering sound, and gazed on them for hours from above and below, and had watched the river foaming over the rapids, then plunging headlong into the dark pool,—and when I had explored the delightful island which divides the falls, where the solitude of the ancient forest is still unbroken, I at last learned by degrees to comprehend the wonders of the scene, and to feel its full magnificence.

Early in the morning after our arrival, I saw from the window of our hotel, on the American side, a long train of white vapory clouds hanging over the deep chasm below the falls. They were slightly tinted by the rays of the rising sun, and blown slowly northwards by a gentle breeze from the pool below the cataract, which was itself invisible from this point of view. No fog was rising from the ground, the sky was clear above; and as the day advanced, and the air grew warm, the vapors all disappeared. This scene reminded me of my first view of Mount Etna from Catania, when I saw dense volumes of steam issuing from the summit of the highest crater in a clear blue sky, which, at the height of more than two miles above the sea, assumed at once the usual shape and hues of clouds in the upper atmosphere. These, too, vanished before noon, as soon as the sun's heat increased.

Etna presents us not merely with an image of the power of subterranean heat, but a record also of the vast period of time during which that power has been exerted. A majestic mountain has been produced by volcanic action, yet the time of which the volcano forms the register, however vast, is found by the geologist to be of inconsiderable amount, even in the modern annals of the earth's history. In like manner, the Falls of Niagara teach us not merely to appreciate the power of moving water, but furnish us at the same time with data for estimating the enormous lapse of ages during which that force has operated. A deep and long ravine has been excavated, and the river has required ages to accomplish the task, yet the same region affords evidence that the sum of these ages is as nothing, and as the work of yesterday, when compared to the antecedent periods, of which there are monuments in the same district.

REDUCED HEIGHT.

It has long been the popular belief, from a mere cursory inspection of this district, that the Niagara once flowed in a shallow valley across the whole platform from the present site of the Falls to the Queenston heights, where it is supposed the cataract was first situated, and that the river has been slowly eating its way backwards through the rocks for a distance of seven miles. According to this hypothesis, the Falls must have had originally nearly twice their present height, and must have been always diminishing in grandeur from age to age, as they will continue to do in future so long as the retrograde movement is prolonged. It becomes, therefore, a matter of no small curiosity and interest to inquire at what rate the work of excavation is now going on, and thus to obtain a measure for calculating how many thousands of years or centuries have been required to hollow out the chasm already excavated.

RECENT PROOFS OF EROSION.

It is an ascertained fact, that the Falls do not remain absolutely stationary at the same point of space, and that they have shifted their position slightly during the last half century. Every observer will also be convinced that the small portion of the great ravine, which has been eroded within the memory of man, is so precisely identical in character with the whole gorge for seven miles below, that the river supplies an adequate cause for executing the task assigned to it, provided we grant sufficient time for its completion. The waters, after cutting through strata of limestone, about fifty feet thick in the rapids, descend perpendicularly at the Falls over another mass of limestone about ninety feet thick, beneath which lie soft shales of equal thickness, continually undermined by the action of the spray driven violently by gusts of wind against the base of the precipice. In consequence of this disintegration, portions of the incumbent rock are left unsupported, and tumble down from time to time, so that the cataract is made to recede southwards. Mr. Bakewell calculated that, in the forty years preceding 1830, the Niagara had been going back at the rate of about a yard annually, but I conceive that one foot per year would be a much more probable conjecture, in which case 35,000 years would have been required for the retreat of the Falls from the escarpment of Queenston to their present site, if we could assume that the retrograde movement had been uniform throughout. This, however, could not have been the case, as at every step in the process of excavation the height of the precipice, the hardness of the materials at its base, and the quantity of fallen matter to be removed, must have varied. At some points it may have receded much faster than at present, at others much slower, and it would be scarcely possible to decide whether its average progress has been more or less rapid than now.

REMNANTS OF AN OLD RIVER-BED.

While we have only meagre historical data, we are fortunately not without geological evidence of the former existence of a channel of the Niagara at a much higher level, before the table-land was intersected by the great ravine. Long before my visit to the Niagara, I had been informed of the existence on Goat Island of beds of gravel and sand containing fluviatile shells, and some account had been given of these by Mr. Hall in his first report. I therefore proposed to him that we should examine these carefully, and see if we could trace any remnants of the same along the edges of the river-cliffs below the Falls. We began by collecting in Goat Island shells of the genera *Unio, Cyclas, Melania, Valvata, Limnea, Planorbis,* and *Helix,* all of recent species, in the superficial deposit. They form regular beds, and numerous individuals of the *Unio* and *Cyclas* have both their valves united. We then found the same formation exactly opposite to the Falls on the top of the cliff (at *d'*, fig. 1.) on the American

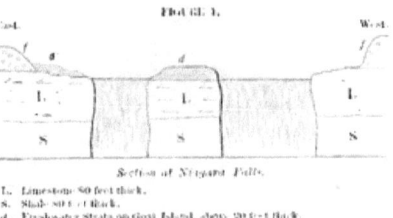

FIG 63. 1.
Section at Niagara Falls.
L. Limestone 80 feet thick.
S. Shale-strata of Black.
d. Freshwater Strata on Goat Island, about 20 feet thick.
d'. Same formation on the American side, with recent bones of Mastodon.
.. Ledge of hard limestone on the Canada side.
f. Ancient drift

side, where two river-terraces, one twelve and the other twenty-four feet above the Niagara, have been cut in the modern deposits. In these we observed the same fossil shells as in Goat Island, and learned that the teeth and other remains of a mastodon, some of which were shown us, had been found thirteen feet below the surface of the soil. We were then taken by our guide to a spot farther north, where similar gravel and sand with fluviatile shells occurred near the edge of the cliff overhanging the ravine, resting on the solid limestone. It was about half a mile below the principal Fall, and extended at some points 300 yards inland, but no farther, for it was then bounded by the bank of more ancient drift (*f,* fig. 1). This deposit precisely occupies the place which the ancient bed and alluvial plain of the Niagara would naturally have filled, if the river once extended farther northwards, at a level sufficiently high to cover the greater part of Goat Island. At that period the ravine could not have existed, and there must have been a barrier, several miles lower down, at or near the whirlpool.

The supposed original channel, through which the waters flowed from Lake Erie to Queenston or Lewiston, was excavated chiefly, but not entirely, in the superficial drift, and the old river-banks cut in this drift are still to be seen facing each other, on both sides of the ravine, for many miles below the Falls. A section of Goat Island from south to north, or parallel to the course of the Niagara (fig. 2), shows that the limestone (B) had been greatly denuded before the fluviatile beds (c) were accumulated, and consequently when the Falls were still several miles below their present site. From this fact I infer that the slope of the river at the rapids was principally due to the original shape of the old channel, and not, as some have conjectured, to modern erosions on the approach of the Falls to the spot.

The observations made in 1841 induced me in the following year to re-examine diligently both sides of the river from the Falls to Lewiston and Queenston, to ascertain if any other patches of the ancient river-bed had escaped destruction. Accordingly, following first the edge of the cliffs on the eastern bank, I discovered, with no small delight, at the summer-house (E, fig. 3), above the whirlpool, a bed of stratified sand and gravel, forty feet thick, containing fluviatile shells in abundance. Fortunately, a few yards from the summer-house a pit had been recently dug for the cellar of a new house to the depth of nine feet in the shelly sand, in which I found shells of the genera *Unio, Cyclas, Melania, Helix,* and *Pupa,* not only identical in species with those which occur in a fresh state in the bed of the Niagara, near the ferry, but corresponding also in the proportionate number of individuals belonging to each species, that of *Cyclas similis,* for example, being the most numerous. The same year I found also a remnant of the old river-bed on the opposite or Ca-

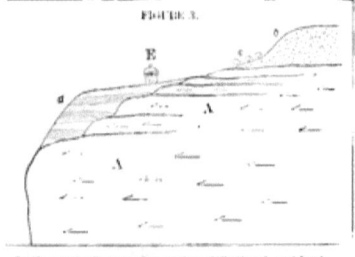

nadian side of the river, about a mile and a half above the whirlpool, or two miles and a half below the Falls. These facts appear conclusive as to the former extension of a more elevated valley, four miles, at least, below the Falls; and at this point the old river-bed must have been so high as to be capable of holding back the waters which covered all the patches of fluviatile sand and gravel, including that of Goat Island. As the table-land or limestone-platform rises gently to the north, and is highest near Queenston, there is no reason to suppose that there was a greater fall in the Niagara when it flowed at its higher level, than now between Lake Erie and the Falls; and according to this view, the old channel might well have furnished the required barrier.

I have stated that on the left, or Canadian bank of the Niagara, below the Falls, I succeeded in detecting sand with freshwater shells at one point only, near the mouth of the muddy river. The ledge of limestone on this side is usually laid bare, or only covered by vegetable mould (as at *e*, fig. 1), until we arrive at the boulder clay (*f. f.* fig. 1), which is sometimes within a few yards of the top of the precipice, and sometimes again retires eighty yards or more from it, being from twenty to fifty feet in height. I also found an old river-bed running through the drift parallel to the Niagara, its course still marked by swamps and ponds, such as we find in all alluvial plains, and only remarkable here because the river now runs at a lower level by 300 feet. This deserted channel occurs between the Muddy River and the Whirlpool, and is 100 yards broad.

THE DEVIL'S HOLE.

There is also a notch or indentation, called the "Devil's Hole," on the right or eastern side of the Niagara, half a mile below the Whirlpool, which deserves notice, for there, I think, there are signs of the Great Cataract having been once situated. A small streamlet, called the "Bloody Run," from a battle fought there with the Indians, joins the Niagara at this place, and has hollowed out a lateral chasm. Ascending the great ravine, we here see, facing us, a projecting cliff of limestone, which stands out forty feet beyond the general range of the river cliff below, and has its flat summit bare and without soil, just as if it had once formed the eastern side of the Great Fall.

RECESSION.

By exploring the banks of the Niagara above the Falls, I satisfied myself that if the river should continue to cut back the ravine still farther southwards, it would leave here and there, near the verge of the precipice and on its islands, strata of sand and loam, with freshwater shells similar to those already described. I collected fossil shells, for example, on the left bank, near the Chippewa River, and learnt that others had been reached, in sinking a well, in 1818, at the south-east end of Grand Island. The situation of such deposits is represented at *a. a* (fig. 4).

The patches of fluviatile strata, therefore, occurring between the old banks of drift (*f. f.* fig. 1) and the precipice, and not having been met with on other parts of the platform at a distance from the Niagara, confirm the theory, previously adopted on independent evidence, of the recession of the Falls from Queenston southwards. The narrowness of the gorge near Queenston, where it is just large enough to contain the rapid current of water, accords well with the same hypothesis, and there is no ground for suspecting that the excavation was assisted by an original rent in the rocks, because there is no fissure at present in the limestone at the Falls, where the moving waters alone have power to cut their way backwards.

I have already remarked that there will always be insuperable difficulties in the way of estimating with precision the rate of the retrogression of the Falls in former ages, because at every step new strata have been successively exposed at the base of the precipice. According to their softer or harder nature, the undermining process must have been accelerated or retarded. This will be understood by reference to the annexed section (fig. 4), where the line b, c, d, represents the present surface of the river along which the Falls have receded. The strata (1, 3 and 7), are of soft materials; the others (2, 4 and 8), which slightly project at their termination in the escarpment, are of a more compact and refractory kind. It has been necessary to exaggerate the southward dip of the strata in this diagram, which is in reality so slight as to be insensible to the eye, being only, as before mentioned, about twenty-five feet in a mile, the river channel sloping in an opposite direction at the rate of fifteen feet in a mile. These two inclinations, taken together, have caused, as Mr. Hall has pointed out in his Survey, a diminution of forty feet in the perpendicular height of the Falls for every mile that they receded southward. By reference to the section, the reader will perceive that when they were situated at the Whirlpool (c) the quartzose sandstone (2), which is extremely hard, was at the base of the precipice, and here the Great Cataract may have remained nearly stationary for ages.

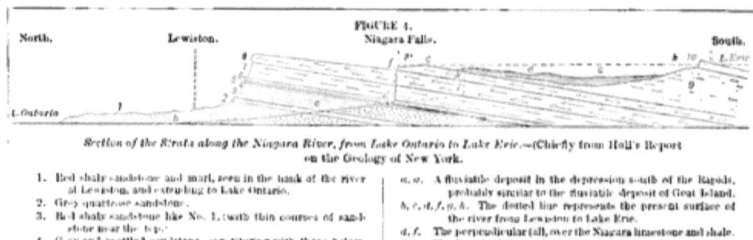

Section of the Strata along the Niagara River, from Lake Ontario to Lake Erie.—(Chiefly from Hall's Report on the Geology of New York.)

1. Red shaly sandstone and marl, seen in the bank of the river at Lewiston, and extending to Lake Ontario.
2. Grey quartzose sandstone.
3. Red shaly sandstone like No. 1, with thin courses of sandstone near the top.
4. Grey and mottled sandstone, constituting with those below, the Medina sandstone.
5. A thin mass of green shale.
6. Compact grey limestone, which, with No. 5, constitutes the Clinton group at this place.
7. Soft argillo-calcareous shale. Niagara shale.
8. Limestone, compact and geodiferous. Niagara limestone.
8'. The upper thin-bedded portion of the Niagara limestone.
9. Onondaga salt group, including the hydraulic limestone, or beds of passage to the next rock.
10. Onondaga and Corniferous limestones, being all the limestones of the Helderberg division which continue so far westward.

$a, a.$ A fluviatile deposit in the depression south of the Rapids, probably similar to the fluviatile deposit of Goat Island.
$b, c, d, f, g, h.$ The dotted line represents the present surface of the river from Lewiston to Lake Erie.
$d, f.$ The perpendicular fall, over the Niagara limestone and shale.
$f, g.$ The Rapids, fifty-two feet, over the upper thin-bedded portion of the Niagara limestone.
$c.$ The Whirlpool.
$i, k.$ The position of the Falls and Rapids after a recession of two miles.

Note. The fainter lines indicate that portion of the rocks which has been already cut through by the Niagara.

The superficial drift or boulder formation is not represented in this section.

Length of section from north to south about twenty-eight miles.

FUTURE RETROCESSION.

In regard to the future retrocession of the Falls, it will be perceived by the same section (fig. 4), that when they have traveled back two miles, or to i, k, the massive limestone (8), now at the top of the Falls, will then be at their base; and its great hardness may, perhaps, effectually stop the excavating process, if it should not have been previously arrested by the descent of large masses of the same rock from the cliff above. It will also appear that the Falls will continually diminish in height, and should they ever reach Lake Erie, they will intersect entirely different strata from those over which they are now thrown.

ORIGIN OF THE FALLS.

The next inquiry into which we are naturally led by our retrospect into the past history of this region, relates to the origin of the Falls. If they were once seven miles northward of their present site, in what manner, and at what geological period, did they first come into existence? In tracing back the series of past events, we have already seen that the last change was the erosion of the great ravine; previously to which occurred the deposition of the freshwater deposit, including fossil shells of recent species, and the bones of the Mastodon. Thirdly, of still older date was the drift or boulder formation which overspreads the whole platform and the face of the escarpment near Queenston, as well as the low country between it and Lake Ontario. Fourthly, the denudation of the line of cliff or escarpment, in which the table-land ends abruptly, preceded the origin of the drift. This drift was of marine origin, and formed when the whole country was submerged beneath the sea. In the region of the Niagara it is stratified, and though no fossils have as yet been detected in it, similar deposits occur in the valley of the St. Lawrence at Montreal, at a height nearly equal to Lake Erie, where fossil shells, of species such as now inhabit the northern seas, lie buried in the drift

It is almost superfluous to affirm that a consideration of the geology of the whole basin of the St. Lawrence and the great lakes can alone entitle us to speculate on the state of things which immediately preceded or accompanied the origin of the Great Cataract. To give even a brief sketch of the various phenomena to which our attention must be directed, in order to solve this curious problem, would require a digression of several chapters. At present the shortest and most intelligible way of explaining the results of my observations and reflections on this subject will be to describe the successive changes in the order in which I imagine them to have happened. The first event then to which we must recur is the superficial waste or denudation of the older stratified rocks (from 1 to 10 inclusive, section, fig. 4), all of which had remained nearly undisturbed and horizontal from the era of their formation beneath the sea to a comparatively modern period. That they were all of marine origin is proved by their imbedded corals and shells. They at length emerged slowly, and portions of their edges were removed by the action of the waves and currents, by which cliffs were formed at successive heights, especially where hard limestones (such as Nos. 10 and 8, fig. 4), at Blackrock and Lewiston, were incumbent on soft shales. After this denudation the whole region was again gradually submerged, and this event took place during the glacial period, at which time the surfaces of the rocks already denuded were smoothed, polished, and furrowed by glacial action, which operated successively at different levels. The country was then buried under a load of stratified and unstratified sand, gravel and erratic blocks, occasionally 80, and in some hollows more than 300, feet deep. An old ravine terminating at St. David's, which intersects the limestone platform of the Niagara, and opens into the great escarpment, illustrates the posteriority of this drift to the epoch when the older rocks were denuded. The period of submergence last alluded to was very modern, for the shells then inhabiting the ocean belonged, almost without exception, to species still living in high northern, and some of them in temperate, latitudes. The next great change was the re-emergence of this country, consisting of the ancient denuded rocks, covered indiscriminately with modern marine drift. The upward movement by which this was accomplished was not sudden and instantaneous, but gradual and intermittent. The pauses by which it was interrupted are marked by ancient beach-lines, ridges, and terraces, found at different heights above the present lakes. These ridges and terraces are partly due to the denudation and re-arrangement of the materials of the drift itself, which had previously been deposited on the platform, the sloping face of the escarpments, and in the basins of the great lakes.

As soon as the table-land between Lakes Erie and Ontario emerged and was laid dry, the river Niagara came into existence, the basin of Lake Ontario still continuing to form part of the sea. From that moment there was a cascade at Queenston of moderate height, which fell directly into the sea. The uppermost limestone and subjacent slate (8 and 7, fig. 4) being exposed, the cataract commenced its retrograde course, while the lower beds in the escarpment (from 6 to 1) were still protected from waste by remaining submerged. A second fall would in due time be caused by the continued rise of the land and the exposure of the hard beds (6 and 4), constituting what is called the Clinton group, together with the soft and easily undermined red shale (3) on which they repose. Finally, a third cascade would in all likelihood be produced by the rise of another hard mass, the quartzose sandstone (2, fig. 4), resting on very destructible red shale (1). Three falls, one above the other, very similar in their geological and geographical position to those actually seen on the river Genesee, at Rochester, would thus be formed. The recession of the uppermost must have been gradually retarded by the thickening of the incumbent limestone (No. 8, fig. 4), in proportion as the falls sawed their way southwards. By this means the second cataract, which would not suffer the same retardation, might overtake it, and the two united would then be retarded by the large quantity of rock to be removed, until the lowest fall would come up to them, and then the whole would be united into one.

LAPSE OF TIME.

The principal events enumerated in the above retrospect, comprising the submergence and re-emergence of the Canadian lake district and valley of the St. Lawrence, the deposition of freshwater strata, and the gradual erosion of a ravine

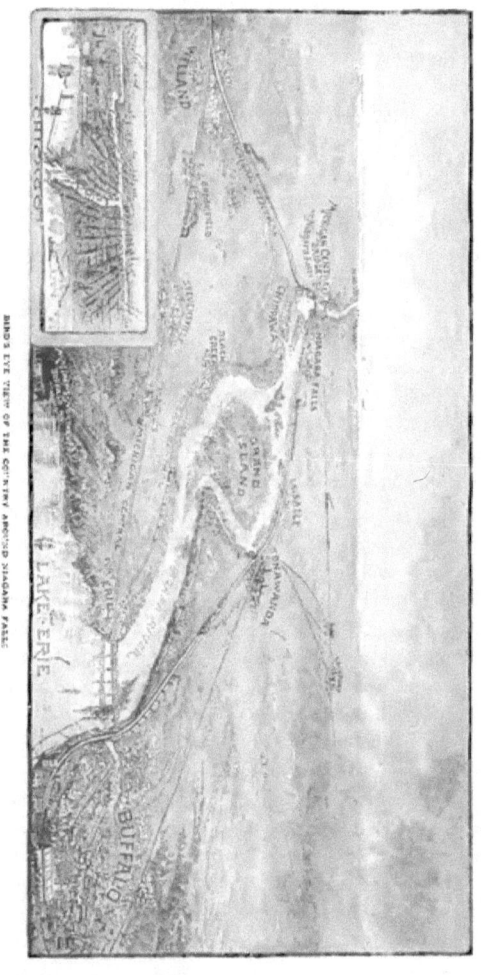

BIRD'S EYE VIEW OF THE COUNTRY AROUND NIAGARA FALLS
(From Lake Erie to Lake Ontario.)

seven miles long, are all so modern in the earth's history as to belong to a period when the marine, the fluviatile, and terrestrial shells were the same, or nearly the same, as those now living. Yet if we fix our thoughts on any one portion of this period—on the lapse of time, for example, required for the recession of the Niagara from the escarpment to the Falls,—how immeasurably great will its duration appear in comparison with the sum of years to which the annals of the human race are limited! Had we happened to discover strata, charged with fluviatile shells of recent species, and enclosing the bones and teeth of a Mastodon, near a river at the bottom of some valley, we might naturally have inferred that the buried quadruped had perished at an era long after the canoes of the Indian hunter had navigated the North American waters. Such an inference might easily have been drawn respecting the fossil tusks of the great elephantine quadruped, which I saw taken out of the shell marl on the banks of the Genesee River near Rochester. But fortunately on the Niagara, we may turn to the deep ravine, and behold therein a chronometer measuring rudely, yet emphatically, the vast magnitude of the interval of years, which separates the present time from the epoch when the Niagara flowed at a higher level several miles further north across the platform. We then became conscious how far the two events before confounded together,—the entombment of the Mastodon, and the date of the first peopling of the earth by man,—may recede to distances almost indefinitely remote from each other.

But, however much we may enlarge our ideas of the time which has elapsed since the Niagara first began to drain the waters of the upper lakes, we have seen that this period was one only of a series, all belonging to the present zoological epoch; or that in which the living testaceous fauna, whether freshwater or marine, had already come into being. If such events can take place while the zoology of the earth remains almost stationary and unaltered, what ages may not be comprehended in those successive tertiary periods during which the Flora and Fauna of the globe have been almost entirely changed! Yet how subordinate a place in the long calendar of geological chronology do the successive tertiary periods themselves occupy! How much more enormous a duration must we assign to many antecedent revolutions of the earth and its inhabitants! No analogy can be found in the natural world to the immense scale of these divisions of past time, unless we contemplate the celestial spaces which have been measured by the astronomer. Some of the nearest of these within the limits of the solar system, as, for example, the orbits of the planets, are reckoned by hundreds of millions of miles, which the imagination in vain endeavors to grasp. Yet one of these spaces, such as the diameter of the earth's orbit, is regarded as a mere unit, a mere infinitesimal fraction of the distance which separates our sun from the nearest star.

By pursuing still farther the same investigations, we learn that there are luminous clouds scarcely distinguishable by the naked eye, but resolvable by the telescope into clusters of stars, which are so much more remote, that the interval between our sun and Sirius may be but a fraction of this larger distance. To regions of space of this higher order in point of magnitude, we may probably compare such an interval of time as that which divides the human epoch from the origin of the coralline limestone over which the Niagara is precipitated at the Falls. Many have been the successive revolutions in organic life, and many the vicissitudes in the physical geography of the globe, and often has sea been converted into land, and land into sea, since that rock was formed. The Alps, the Pyrenees, the Himalaya, have not only begun to exist as lofty mountain chains, but the solid materials of which they are composed have been slowly elaborated beneath the sea within the stupendous interval of ages here alluded to.

The geologist may muse and speculate on these events until, filled with awe and admiration, he forgets the presence of the mighty cataract itself, and no longer sees the rapid motion of its waters, nor hears their sound, as they fall into the deep abyss. But whenever his thoughts are recalled to the present, the tone of his mind,—the sensations awakened in his soul, will be found to be in perfect harmony with the grandeur and beauty of the glorious scene which surrounds him.

PAST AND FUTURE.

PROFESSOR TYNDALL.

WE HAVE now to consider the genesis and proximate destiny of the Falls of Niagara. We may open our way to this subject by a few preliminary remarks upon erosion. Time and intensity are the main factors of geological change, and they are in a certain sense convertible. A feeble force acting through long periods, and an intense force acting through short ones, may produce approximately the same results. To Dr. Hooker I have been indebted for some samples of stones, the first examples of which were picked up by Mr. Hackworth on the shores of Lyell's Bay, near Wellington, in New Zealand. They have been described by Mr. Travers in the Transactions of the New Zealand Institute. Unacquainted with their origin, you would certainly ascribe their forms to human workmanship. They resemble flint knives and spear-heads, being apparently chiseled off into faces with as much attention to symmetry as if a tool guided by human intelligence had passed over them. But no human instrument has been brought to bear upon these stones. They have been wrought into their present shape by the wind-blown sand of Lyell's Bay. Two winds are dominant here, and they in succession urged the sand against opposite sides of the stone; every little particle of sand chipped away its infinitesimal bit of stone, and in the end sculptured these singular forms.

EFFECTS OF THE SAND BLAST.

The Sphinx of Egypt is nearly covered up by the sand of the desert. The neck of the Sphinx is partly cut across, not, as I am assured by Mr. Huxley, by ordinary weathering, but by the eroding action of the fine sand blown against it. In these cases nature furnishes us with hints which may be taken advantage of in art; and this action of sand has recently been turned to extraordinary account in the United States. When in Boston, I was taken by Mr. Josiah Quincy to see the action of the *sand-blast*. A kind of hopper containing fine silicious sand was connected with a reservoir of compressed air, the pressure being variable at pleasure. The hopper ended in a long slit, from which the sand was blown. A plate of glass was placed beneath this slit, and caused to pass slowly under it; it came out perfectly depolished, with a bright opalescent glimmer, such as could only be produced by the most careful grinding. Every little particle of sand urged against the glass, having all its energy concentrated on the point of impact, formed there a little pit, the depolished surface consisting of innumerable hollows of this description. But this was not all. By protecting certain portions of the surface and exposing others, figures and tracery of any required form could be etched upon the glass. The figures of open iron-work could thus be copied, while the wire-gauze placed over the glass produced a reticulated pattern. But it required no such resisting substance as iron to shelter the glass. The patterns of the finest lace could thus be reproduced; the delicate filaments of the lace itself offering a sufficient protection.

All these effects have been obtained with a simple model of the sand-blast devised for me by my assistant. A fraction of a minute suffices to etch upon glass a rich and beautiful lace pattern. Any yielding substance may be employed to protect the glass. By immediately diffusing the shock of the particle, such substances practically destroy the local erosive power. The hand can bear without inconvenience a sand-shower which would pulverize glass. Etchings executed on glass with suitable kinds of ink are accurately worked out by the sand-blast. In fact, within certain limits, the harder the surface, the greater is the concentration of the shock, and the more effectual is the erosion. It is not necessary that the sand should be the harder substance of the two; corundum, for example, is much harder than quartz; still, quartz-sand can not only demolish, but actually blow a hole through a plate of corundum. Nay, glass may be depolished by the impact of fine shot; the grains in this case bruising the glass before they have time to flatten and turn their energy into heat.

EROSIVE POWER OF RIVERS.

This power of erosion, so strikingly displayed when sand is urged by air, renders us better able to conceive its action when urged by water. The erosive power of a river is vastly augmented by the solid matter carried along with it. Sand or pebbles caught in a river vortex can wear away the hardest rock; "pot-holes" and deep cylindrical shafts being thus produced. An extraordinary instance of this kind of erosion is to be seen in the Val Tournanche, above the village of this name. The gorge at Handeck has been thus cut out. Such waterfalls were once frequent in the valleys of Switzerland; for hardly any valley is without one or more transverse barriers of resisting material, over which the river flowing through the valley once fell as a cataract. Near Pontresina in the Engadin, there is such a case, the hard gneiss being now worn away to form a gorge through which the river from the Morteratsch glacier rushes. The barrier of the Kirchet above Meyringen is also a case in point. Behind it was a lake, derived from the glacier of the Aar, and over the barrier the lake poured its excess of water. Here the rock being limestone was in great part dissolved, but added to this we had the action of the solid particles carried along by the water, each of which, as it struck the rock, chipped it away like the particles of the sand-blast. Thus by solution and mechanical erosion the great chasm of the Fensteraar-Schlucht was formed. It is demonstrable that the water which flows at the bottom of such deep fissures once flowed at the level of what is now their edges, and tumbled down the lower faces of the barriers. Almost every valley in Switzerland furnishes examples of this kind; the untenable hypothesis of earthquakes, once so readily resorted in accounting for these gorges, being now for the most part abandoned. To produce the Canyons of Western America no other cause is needed than the integration of effects individually infinitesimal

ORIGIN AND PROGRESS OF THE CATARACT.

And now we come to Niagara. Soon after Europeans had taken possession of the country, the conviction appears to have arisen that the deep channel of the river Niagara below the falls had been excavated by the cataract. In Mr. Bakewell's "Introduction to Geology," the prevalence of this belief has been referred to; it is expressed thus by Prof. Joseph Henry in the Transactions of the Albany Institute: "In viewing the position of the falls and the features of the country round, it is impossible not to be impressed with the idea that this great natural raceway has been formed by the continued action of the irresistible Niagara, and that the falls, beginning at Lewiston, have, in the course of ages, worn back the rocky strata to their present site." The same view is advocated by Sir Charles Lyell, by Mr. Hall, by M. Agassiz, by Prof. Ramsay, indeed by almost all of those who have inspected the place.

A connected image of the origin and progress of the cataract is easily obtained. Walking northward from the village of Niagara Falls by the side of the river, we have to our left the deep and comparatively narrow gorge through which the Niagara flows. The bounding cliffs of this gorge are from 300 to 350 feet high. We reach the whirlpool, trend to the northeast, and after a little time gradually resume our northward course. Finally, at about seven miles from the present Falls, we come to the edge of a declivity which informs us that we have been hitherto walking on table-land. Some hundreds of feet below us is a comparatively level plain, which stretches to Lake Ontario. The declivity marks the end of the precipitous gorge of the Niagara. Here the river escapes from its steep mural boundaries, and in a widened bed pursues its way to the lake which finally receives its waters.

IN THE PAST.

The fact that in historic times, even within the memory of man, the fall has sensibly receded, prompts the question, how far has recession gone? At what point did the ledge which thus continually creeps backwards begin its retrograde course? To minds disciplined in such researches the answer has been and will be, at the precipitous declivity which crossed the Niagara from Lewiston on the American to Queenston on the Canadian side. Over this transverse barrier the united affluents of all the upper lakes once poured their waters, and here the work of erosion began. The dam, moreover, was demonstrably of sufficient height to cause the river above it to submerge Goat Island; and this would perfectly account for the finding by Mr. Hall, Sir Charles Lyell, and others, in the sand and gravel of the island, the same fluviatile shells as are now found in the Niagara river higher up. It would also account for those deposits along the sides of the river, the discovery of which enabled Lyell, Hall, and Ramsay to reduce to demonstration the popular belief that the Niagara once flowed through a shallow valley.

The physics of the problem of excavation, which I made clear to my mind before quitting Niagara, are revealed by a close inspection of the present Horse-Shoe Fall. Here we see evidently that the greatest weight of water bends over the very apex of the Horse-Shoe. In a passage in his excellent chapter on Niagara Falls, Mr. Hall alludes to this fact. Here we have the most copious and the most violent whirling of the shattered liquid; here the most powerful eddies recoil against the shale. From this portion of the fall, indeed, the spray sometimes rises without solution of continuity to the region of the clouds, becoming gradually more attenuated, and passing finally through the condition of true cloud into invisible vapor, which is sometimes reprecipitated higher up. All the phenomena point distinctly to the centre of the river as the place of greatest mechanical energy, and from the centre the vigor of the Fall gradually dies away towards the sides. The horse-shoe form, with the concavity facing downwards, is an obvious and necessary consequence of this action. Right along the middle of the river the apex of the curve pushes its way backwards, cutting along the centre a deep and comparatively narrow groove, and draining the sides as it passes them. Hence the remarkable discrepancy between the widths of the Niagara above and below the Horse-Shoe. All along its course, from Lewiston Heights to its present position, the form of the Fall was probably that of a horse-shoe, for this is merely the expression of the greater depth, and consequently greater excavating power, of the centre of the river. The gorge, moreover, varies in width as the depth of the centre of the ancient river varied, being narrowest where that depth was greatest.

EROSIVE POWER OF THE HORSE-SHOE FALL.

The vast comparative erosive energy of the Horse-Shoe Fall, comes strikingly into view when it and the American Fall are compared together. The American branch of the upper river is cut at a right angle by the gorge of the Niagara. Here the Horse-Shoe Fall was the real excavator. It cut the rock and formed the precipice over which the American Fall tumbles. But since its formation, the erosive action of the American Fall has been almost nil, while the Horse-Shoe has cut its way for five hundred yards across the end of Goat Island, and is doubling back to excavate a channel parallel to the length of the island. This point, I have just learned, has not escaped the acute observation of Prof. Ramsay, whose words are: "Where the body of water is small in the American Fall, the edge has only receded a few yards (where most eroded) during the time that the Canadian Fall has receded from the north corner of Goat Island to the inner-most curve of the Horse-Shoe Fall." The river bends; the Horse-Shoe immediately accommodates itself to the bending, and will follow implicitly the direction of the deepest water in the upper stream. The flexibility of the gorge, if I may use the term, is determined by the flexibility of the river channel above it. Were the Niagara above the Fall sinuous, the gorge would obediently follow its sinuosities. Once suggested, no doubt geographers will be able to point out many examples of this action. The Zambesi is thought to present a great difficulty to the erosion theory, because of the sinuosity of the chasm below the Victoria Falls. But assuming the basalt to be of tolerably uniform texture, had the river been examined before the formation of this sinuous channel, the present zigzag course of the gorge below the Fall could, I am persuaded, have been predicted while the sounding of the present river would enable us to predict the course to be pursued by the erosion in the future.

But not only has the Niagara river cut the gorge; it has carried away the chips of its own workshop. The shale being probably crumpled is easily carried away. But at the base of the fall we find the huge boulders already described, and by some means or other these are removed down the river. The ice which fills the gorge in winter, and which grapples with the boulders, has been regarded as the transporting agent. Probably it is so to some extent. But erosion acts without ceasing on the abutting points of the boulders, thus withdrawing their support and urging them gradually down the river. Solution also does its portion of the work. That solid matter is carried down is proved by the difference of depth between the Niagara river and Lake Ontario, where the river enters it. The depth fails from seventy-two feet to twenty feet, in consequence of the deposition of solid matter caused by the diminished motion of the river.

THE FUTURE.

In conclusion, we may say a word regarding the proximate future of Niagara. At the rate of excavation assigned to it by Sir Charles Lyell, namely, a foot a year, five thousand years or so will carry the Horse-Shoe Fall far higher than Goat Island. As the gorge recedes it will drain, as it has hitherto done, the banks right and left of it, thus leaving a nearly level terrace between Goat Island and the edge of the gorge. Higher up it will totally drain the American branch of the river; the channel of which in due time will become cultivable land. The American Fall will then be transformed into a dry precipice, forming a simple continuation of the cliffy boundary of the Niagara. At the place occupied by the fall at this moment we shall have the gorge enclosing a right angle, a second whirlpool being the consequence of this. To those who visit Niagara a few millenniums hence I leave the verification of this prediction. All that can be said is, that if the causes now in action continue to act, it will prove itself literally true.

THE CATARACT BY ELECTRIC LIGHT.

GRATUITOUS ASSERTIONS.

J. M. DUNCAN.

THE FALLS of Niagara are among those phenomena in the external world, from which speculatists have spun a cobweb theory of the earth, proving or intended to prove

"That he who made it, and revealed its date
To Moses, was mistaken in its age."

There is every reason to believe from the aspect of the banks, and the character of the surrounding country above and below the Falls, that the river has at some former period scooped out the channel, through the solid limestone, from Queenston, about seven miles below, to the position of the cataracts. Below Queenston, the ground on both sides of the river is very nearly of the same level with the banks of lake Ontario, but at that town it rises with a sudden and steep slope crossing the river at right angles to its channel, and continuing gradually to increase in elevation, till it attains to the height of lake Erie. At Queenston the inner surface of the banks first becomes precipitous and broken; and mineralogists of whose accuracy and fidelity there can be no doubt, have ascertained, by minute inspection, that the strata, (limestone above, and sandstone below, with forty feet interposing of exceedingly friable slate,) on the opposite sides of the river correspond exactly with each other, and scarcely vary to the situation of the present Falls. From these premises it has been concluded, that the waters of the Niagara formerly ran down the face of the heights of Queenston,—that the rocky material at last gave way under the continued attrition, and that the cataract gradually worked its way backward, till it separated into two at the present position. Not only so, but that this process has continued with the most unvarying regularity, accomplishing very nearly the same number of inches in the same space of time. This backward motion however, if any such there be, is at present amazingly slow, and it is therefore decided, with unhesitating certainty and coolness, that the world must have existed, and the waters of the Niagara have been at work, for a much larger period than six thousand years.

With the same facility of hypothesis and assertion, they have decided upon its future as easily as upon its past operations. It is inevitably certain, we are assured, that it will gradually saw its way twenty miles farther and drain lake Erie, and going backward three hundred miles, take up its temporary residence below Detroit. It is needless for us at present to pursue it any farther.

But if we grant, that there was a time when the water from lake Erie first made a breach in Queenston heights, these theorists cannot refuse, that there must have been a previous time when no breach as yet existed. If so, where then was the outlet of lake Erie? By what channel did the waters of the great chain of western lakes, above Ontario, find a passage to the ocean? If these lakes did not then exist, and if they and their outlet were the simultaneous result of some mighty terraqueous convulsion, may it not be as reasonably concluded that the whole channel of the Niagara, from the present Falls to Queenston, was ploughed out by the same revolutionizing struggle—and that in place of being the operation of thousands of years, it may have been the work of a month or perhaps of a day? Upon this supposition it is not difficult to account for the present position of the Falls; below them the channel is comparatively narrow and confined, and the current must have raged, as indeed it still does, with much more fury and effect than where it is less pent up. At the Falls it is divided by an island into two arms, each wider than the channel below; and farther up it is diffused over a still more ample surface, peacefully winding round islands of various sizes, or smoothly expanding into a kind of bay. Within the semicircular outline also of the present Falls, a kind of basin is embraced, in which the water foams and whirls in great agitation, but in which it has space to subside into smoothness before breaking on the bank; and it is comparatively tranquil at a short distance below.

In a word, the assertions which have been made respecting the gradual retrocession of the Falls, seem to be altogether gratuitous. It is possible that some partial change may take place in the outline of the great Fall; some piece of rock may give way, as was the case in the bank below, but there seems not the slightest reason to believe, either that the change has hitherto been incessant and gradual, or that it will hereafter be so. The earliest accounts which were given of them by European writers are obviously and grossly fabulous, describing them as seven or eight hundred feet high, and a mile and a half broad; but the first which were at all authentic correspond remarkably, at the distance of a century, with the present aspect of the cataracts.

The measurement of the Falls has been variously stated. The Horse-Shoe Fall may be stated at about 150 feet in height; its width can only be approximated, but following the curve it is generally estimated at about 2,000 feet. However, it has but a remote resemblance to that which gives it its name; it forms an irregular segment of a circle, with a very deep angular gash near the center. In this gap the water glides over the edge of the rock with most crystalline smoothness, while at either extremity it breaks into snow-white foam at the very edge. The American Fall is about 1,100 feet in extreme width. Its height is 165 feet. The brow of Goat Island is about 980 feet in breadth. The whole extent therefore of the concave, from the farther extremity of the American Fall to the Table Rock, following the line of the cataracts is, according to this calculation, very nearly 4,000 feet.

HORSE-SHOE FALLS FROM THE FERRY ROAD.

NIAGARA FALLS, ONTARIO.

THIS VILLAGE, formerly known as Clifton, extends along the Canada shore of Niagara River, from the Upper-Rapids at the Horse-Shoe Fall, to the railroad Suspension bridge, a distance of over two miles. The most interesting portion of the village lies in the immediate vicinity of the Falls, and a beautiful prospect can be enjoyed at almost any point on Main street, the only street along the river bank upon which buildings are erected. The Canada shore can claim one point over all other localities around the Falls, in being the only place, at present, where a good view of the Cataract can be had without the payment of admittance fees. It is, however, hoped that the creation of the International Park may take place at an early date, and secure similar privileges on the American side. From Niagara Falls station, the omnibuses and carriages of the Michigan Central Transfer Company convey passengers to any point on the Canadian or American side, at the rate of fifty cents for each passenger and usual amount of baggage. This Company has been organized for the protection of the traveling public, and from the gentlemanly agents in charge, every one can feel sure to receive courteous replies and most reliable information. The tourist, wishing to select a temporary abiding place on the Canada side, will find several well-kept hotels, at prices varying according to accommodations desired. The largest and most commodious of these is the Clifton House, which has been open to the public for more than forty years, and has an established reputation. The Prospect House is almost on the verge of the Falls being located at Table Rock.

The Brunswick House, located midway between the houses above mentioned, immediately opposite the Center Fall, furnishes a pleasant stopping place, with all its appointments complete, and well calculated to promote the comfort of its patrons. It is indeed a desirable stopping place, the terms being moderate and the fare excellent. It has ever been the aim of M. Kick, its present proprietor, to keep a first-class hotel, suited to the needs of visitors desirous of witnessing the grand spectacle of Niagara without incurring heavy expenses, and as such, "The Brunswick" has fully established its right to be regarded as a success. Seeing is believing

VILLAGE OF NIAGARA FALLS, N. Y.

On the American Side

THE VILLAGE of Niagara Falls, N. Y., was incorporated on July 6th, 1848, and contains to-day a population of nearly four thousand inhabitants. It boasts of several hotels, large stores, churches to the number of six, and has one of the largest paper mills in the State of New York. The main business street of the village is Falls street, on which may be found hardware, dry goods, and almost all the business of the place; the post-office is located about the center of the street, and at its foot may be seen a Soldier's Monument. In summer time the streets present quite an animated appearance; they are broad and well kept, and abound in fine shade trees; especially may this be said of First street, on which four churches are situated in close proximity to each other. Buffalo street contains some fine residences. The hotels are prominent features of the place.

The Cataract House, dates its existence back to the year 1825. It is a handsome building, possessing all the modern improvements, eligibly located on the very bank of the river, over the Rapids, above the Falls, and receives liberal patronage from the most opulent guests. It is, in every respect, a first-class hotel.

The International Hotel has accommodation for 600 guests. It is a mammoth fire-proof building, and, borrowing a quotation from a Niagara Guide Book, "its conveniences are not intended for the use of the poorest of Niagara's visitors."

The Hotel Kaltenbach, located within a few steps east of the Cataract House, and in full view of the American Rapids, can be classed as one of the fine hotels at the Falls. A neater, cosier, pleasanter, and more home-like abiding place cannot be found anywhere. The building is a new, handsome three-story brick structure, after the gothic style, and contains thirty sleeping-rooms. This house has put

in practice a feature worthy of imitation at summer resorts, and specially at Niagara Falls. Its rates are posted upon the door of each room—$3.00 per day—and are uniform to all comers. Mr. Kaltenbach deserves much from the traveling public, and it is only to be regretted that the limited size of the building does not permit the entertainment of hundreds of daily visitors. The "Kaltenbach" is open summer and winter. It commands the enviable patronage of the best class of tourists.

The Spencer House is conveniently situated opposite the New York Central depot. It is kept open the year around, and ranks among the best hotels at Niagara. The Niagara House is largely patronized by commercial travelers and tourists. It possesses comfortable appointments with pleasant surroundings. It is open at all seasons of the year. The Goat Island House, situated at the Island bridge entrance, at the edge of the Rapids, offers also good inducements to visitors The Pacific Hotel ranks among the good hotels of the place and is kept open during the entire year. Other Hotels there are on this side, of which the limits of this work forbid even a  mention. The press is well represented by the Daily and Weekly Gazette, under the management of Peter A. Porter. To-day, Niagara Falls is popularly known as a fashionable and inviting place of resort, only. The town of the future, however, is destined to be ranged among the most important of our manufacturing marts. The immense water-power, which can be utilized so easily, has begun to attract the attention of capitalists. The projected International Park will contribute materially to the industrial advancement and progress of the town, its object being not to drive away manufacturers, but simply to exclude them from the immediate proximity of the cataract.

The much abused and villified Niagara hackman is, of course, one of the prominent features of the street. To him might properly apply the description of "Bill Warnick," the hackman of the Indianapolis Herald.

> He allus kept his eyes ahead
>   Whichever way he went.
> He was up in his profession—he
>   Could buzz a passenger
> Successful half a square, right through
>   The winder of a kyer,
> And he knowed the human way so well,
>   He never missed a fit
> When it came to making charges
>   And securin' his perkisit.

1—BIDDLE S STAIRS. 2—SPIRAL STAIRCASE AT TABLE ROCK.   —SUSPENSION BRIDGE
  —BRIDGE TO MOSS ISLAND.   5—AMERICAN RAPIDS.

RETROSPECT.

L. BEVILLE.

AT THE beginning of the nineteenth century, in order to visit the great and wonderful Falls of Niagara, it was still a venturesome enterprise to make a path through the mazes of the unfrequented wilderness which served them as a shield and frame. To-day all this is vastly changed, and the annual tide of visitors setting toward these famous falls seems as ample as their floods. In the double silence of night and of the virgin forest, it was doubtless possible, as the writers of a preceding generation assure us, to hear the dull roar of the cataract ten miles away, but to-day the hissing of steam-engines which rush over the water and glide over the land in every direction, the sound of the forges, the shouts and vociferations of the carters and coachmen, and the numberless and incessant cries and clamors which rise from the farm-houses, shops and villas which line the river banks, form a concert in which the voice of the flood at a distance is lost like that of an artist in the orchestra of an imperial academy of music. And, besides, on the American side, a city—a real city, under the name of a village—has sprung up, with long, straight, broad streets, and six churches, and a dozen elegant hotels, on the rocky shelf over which the river leaps. The primeval forest, the virgin solitude has been metamorphosed into gardens laid out with more or less taste, into lawns carpeted with well-kept velvet turf, and beds filled with rare flowers. And the shops, saw mills, and paper mills established near the falls, driven by water taken from them and devoted to the service of industry, reminds one involuntarily of Pegasus entangled in vulgar harness and subjected to the switch of the jockey or the whip of the carter. For the rest, simple souls who are still moved by nature, by the sacred poetry of the earth, may congratulate themselves that they can see Niagara even as it is, for if it had entered into the head of some enterprising speculator, to divide and sub-divide it, to parcel it out into park ponds and puddles, garden fountains, or even globes for gold-fish, he might have done that also.

A BRIEF GUIDE
—TO—
NIAGARA FALLS AND VICINITY.

COMPILED FROM PILGRIMS' NOTES.

READER, the pilgrim stands entranced and lingers on the platform at the station of Falls View, on the Canada side. He hesitates to advance farther in his explorations, in fear of destroying the deeply-rooted impressions left upon all his senses at the first sight of that wondrous vision of Niagara, which defies at once description and analysis, and excites by turns, ideas of grandeur, beauty, terror, power, sublimity. But remembering his bounden duty to you, he wends his way, leisurely, to the little Canadian village lying immediately under the brow of the hill, and soon reaches the river bank.

GENERAL VIEW.—From the bank just below the Clifton House there is a fine panoramic view of both Falls. The larger cataract stretching from shore to shore is the Canadian or Horse-Shoe Fall, whilst the smaller one is the American. This view embraces the entire contour of the Cataract from the northern point of the American Fall to the Canadian shore at Table-Rock.

AMERICAN FALLS—FRONT VIEW.—A few steps farther, and from a small platform on the ledge opposite the Brunswick House, there is a most interesting front view of the American and Center Falls. The Rapids above, the church spires of the American village showing through the trees, the islands in the river, the rocks at the foot of the Falls upon which the descending torrent breaks into spray, all contribute to the magnificence of the picture.

TABLE ROCK exists only in name, and in the interest which attaches to its site. It was a truly magnificent crag, overhanging the fearful abyss, and it constituted one of the wonders of the place. The overhanging Table fell in 1850, and its remains stand in a huge mass of rock at the edge of the river below the bank. It extends along the bank to the very junction with the Horse-Shoe Fall, and the view from it is full of sublimity.

HORSE-SHOE FALL.—Here we are at the edge of the famous Cataract. The pencil nor the pen can do justice to the scene. The silent and still picture wants the motion and the sound of that stupendous rush of waters. An ever-rising column of spray, crowned with prismatic glory, spires upward from the foaming gulf below. This spectacle alone is worth a pilgrimage of several thousand miles to see. The depth of the water in the center is more than 20 feet, as proven by an experiment made with the unseaworthy vessel, "Michigan," sent over the Falls in 1827.

This Fall is 1900 feet across with a drop of 158 feet and fully fifteen hundred million cubic feet of water pass over the ledge every hour. The name "Horse-Shoe" is hardly true to the present shape, which is now more nearly rectangular. The horse-shoe curve has been marred by the falling of portions of the cliff at various times, until its original symmetry has nearly departed.

THE SPIRAL STAIRCASE, firmly anchored to the rocky banks at the north end of Table-Rock, descends the perpendicular face of the cliff and leads under Table-Rock and to the foot of the Horse-Shoe Fall. Dresses and guides must be obtained to pass

BELOW TABLE-ROCK AND UNDER THE FALL.—The view here is grand in an awful degree. An indescribable feeling of awe steals over us, and we are more than ever impressed with the tremendous magnificence of Niagara, as we gaze upwards at the frowning cliff that seems tottering to its fall, and pass under the thick curtain of water—so near that it seems as if we could touch it—and hear the hissing spray, and are stunned by the deafening roar that issues from the misty vortex at our feet. The precipice of the Horse-Shoe Fall rises perpendicularly to a height of 90 feet; at our feet the cliff descends about 70 feet into a turmoil of bursting foam; in front is the liquid curtain which, though ever passing onward, never unveils this wildest of Nature's caverns.

Emerging from our expedition into the cavernous recess of the Great Fall, we now gaze from Table Rock at the

CANADIAN RAPIDS ABOVE THE FALLS, full before us, sweeping down, multitudinous, apparently illimitable, the white foaming crests drawn sharply against the horizon.

Continuing the road, we cross to CEDAR ISLAND, and following the GRAND RAPIDS DRIVE, one of the pleasantest around Niagara, along the Canadian Rapids, we reach the CLARK HILL ISLANDS, five in number, connected to the main land at either end, by the elegant suspension bridges, "Castor" and "Pollux." CYNTHIA ISLAND stands on our left, and immediately opposite, across a wild branch of the river, the cottage erected over the renowned BURNING SPRING, where, through a fissure in the rock, an inflammable sulphurous gas comes up.

From the bluff above the Burning Spring, a magnificent view is had of the Rapids and the river, and also of

NAVY ISLAND, over three hundred acres in area. The island is a British possession, and in 1837 was made the rendezvous of the Canadian Patriots in open rebellion against the authorities of the Dominion.

Retracing our steps, we notice, passing through the village,

THE MUSEUM BUILDING, which contains a collection of natural and artificial curiosities gathered from the various corners of the earth, and tastefully arranged for display.

Our objective point now is the American Side, and in three or four minutes we reach the bank below the Clifton. Here we have a choice of two methods in crossing the river. We may descend the bank and cross by the ferry, or may go over the New Suspension Bridge. Adopting the former, we descend the path, and at the water's edge find

THE FERRY.—We commit ourselves to the little boat and are soon dancing on the agitated waters, gazing in profound silence at the Falls. This crossing affords most vivid impressions of the majesty and immensity of the Cataract. The brawny boatman handles his oars dexterously, and in a few minutes we are landed close at the foot of the American Fall.

Passing through a tunnel-like shed and donning an oil-skin dress, we emerge onto the rocks into a storm of spray, and stand upon

THE HURRICANE BRIDGE, from which may be seen a tremendous ghost of mist, forming heavy clouds fringed with all the brilliant colors of the rainbow. The scene is wild and overpowering. Looking up to the towering crest of the stupendous cataract, the immense mass of waters seems to pour down from the skies. We pass now to

THE SHADOW OF THE ROCK, the name given to a recess behind the Fall itself, which extends nearly to the center of the Fall, and is filled with the dashing spray perpetually rising from the cauldron of waters. The roar of the cataract echoes and re-echoes within this chamber, the effect being heightened by the compression of the air.

To reach the Table-land above we pass through the dressing rooms, where we cast off our mariner's suit and are ready for a trip up

THE INCLINED RAILWAY.—A tunnel has been cut from the cliffs to the margin of the river, at an angle of about thirty degrees, and within it is built the railway, by the side of which is a flight of stairs, numbering 290 steps. The cars are raised and lowered by machinery, and are so arranged that one ascends while the other descends.

PROSPECT POINT is on the very verge of the Fall, at the point where its mighty waters descend in one solemn unbroken mass into a gulf of spray rising in clouds from the tortured waves beneath, and driven about by the gusts, till sometimes the whole river and the opposite shores are momentarily concealed. As this misty curtain is withdrawn, the whole scene is disclosed. Immediately in front is the American Fall, its waters almost in reach of the outstretched hand, beyond this Luna Island and the wooded steps of Goat Island, while to the right stretches in wonderful magnificence the sublime curve of the Horse-Shoe Fall; and up the stream the foaming rapids greet the vision.

PROSPECT PARK extends all around us, a remnant of the natural forest. Cool, shady walks run in all directions, the air is full of the fragrance of wild blossoms, rustic seats at intervals furnish delightful resting places and convenient positions to gaze at the scenery. When the shades of night envelop the earth in darkness, electric lights pour their brilliant rays upon the scene, infusing the spray clouds with gorgeous rainbow tints and brilliantly illuminating the rolling waters. An Art Gallery, Concert Hall, Fountains, Bazaar, and other objective points of entertainment, are provided to engage the attention of visitors.

Leaving the Park at its south-eastern corner we find on our right the toll-gate of

GOAT ISLAND BRIDGE.—This structure is remarkable from the fact that it spans one of the most turbulent of any known rapids. It was first built as a frail wooden structure in 1817, by Judge Porter, and was soon carried away. It was replaced by a stronger one, which stood from 1818 to 1856, when it was removed, and the present elegant structure substituted. The foundations are heavy oaken cribs, filled with stone and plated with iron. The bridge itself is of iron, in four arches, each of ninety feet span, making a total length of three hundred and sixty feet. Its width is twenty-seven feet, comprising a double carriage-way, with footway on either side. Here is the finest outlook on

THE AMERICAN RAPIDS ABOVE THE FALLS, which viewed from this point present that same appearance of plunging from the sky which renders the view of the Canadian Rapids from the Canada shore so impressive.

SHIP AND BRIG ISLANDS stem the current a little above the bridge and are two small wooded isles of rare beauty. It needs but little effort of the imagination to fancy them vessels under full press of sail, endeavoring to sheer out of the current that hurries them inevitably down. Ship Island was once accessible by a bridge connecting it with Bath Island. It was swept away and has not been rebuilt.

BATH ISLAND, one of the group of islands which stud the rapids upon the American side, above the cataract, is the first on our way. It contains about two acres, and its former scenes of loveliness have disappeared to make room for the various buildings and sheds of a large paper-mill. Looking down the river are several small islets, the first two of which are named Chapin and Robinson Islands.

CHAPIN ISLAND received its name from that of a workman who fell into the rapids while repairing the Goat Island bridge, was hurled to its shores, and notwithstanding the imminent peril of the undertaking was rescued by Joel R. Robinson.

ROBINSON ISLAND is named after the intrepid navigator of Niagara's troubled waters, whose brave feats of daring in rescuing life and property, should immortalize his name.

Crossing by a bridge of a single span, at the south end of Bath Island, we are

On GOAT ISLAND, into a shady forest, almost in its primeval simplicity, a most lovely and romantic spot of ground, affording a cool retreat in summer from the noon-day heat, beneath the dense foliage of trees abounding there, upon the trunks of which are inscribed various names and dates showing that visits were here made as early as 1769. It was, in ancient times, one of the favorite burying-grounds of the Indians. It owes its singular name to the fact that some goats placed there to pasture in 1779, perished from the cold during the ensuing winter. This Island, forming on one side a part of the precipice, commences near the head of the Rapids almost in the center of the river, dividing it so as to form the two main portions of the Falls. It covers an extent of seventy acres.

On reaching the Island we have taken the first road leading to the right and arrive at the northwest part, upon a narrow ridge, called from its shape,

HOG'S BACK from which we gain one of the finest views of the American Falls. Right in front is the small Center Fall, and the foot-bridge which leads to Luna Island, with its dwarfed and stunted trees; beyond is the serrated line of the American Fall; while the distance is filled up with the receding lines of the banks of the river below.

Descending the steps in front of us, we cross a pretty and substantial bridge over the stream that forms the Center Fall and land upon

LUNA ISLAND, a pleasant little islet well worthy of a visit. Its name came to it in connection with the weird and pleasing appearance of the Lunar bows, visible there.

THE THREE PROFILES are an irregular projection of that portion of the precipice which is formed by the west side of Luna Island, and are almost under the American Fall. They obtain their name from their remarkable likeness to three human faces.

THE CENTER FALL over which we pass on our way to and from Goat Island, although a mere ribbon of white water when seen from a short distance in contrast with the Great Falls, is by no means unworthy of notice. It is 100 feet wide, and a very graceful sheet of water. A few paces bring us to the entrance of

BIDDLE'S STAIRS erected in 1829, by Mr. Biddle, president of the United States Bank. They are firmly secured to the cliff, quite safe, and 80 feet high. The total descent from the top of the bank to the bottom is 185 feet. Descending the stairs we take the pathway to the right, and having previously donned a water-proof dress are prepared for a visit to

THE CAVE OF THE WINDS, which lies behind the Center Fall. The Cave is 100 feet high by 100 deep and 160 long, and its existence is due to the action of the waters upon the shale, leaving the more solid limestone rock overhanging. A visitor, whose impressions appeared in Harper's Magazine years ago, gives a most graphic description: "Close by the entrance you look down into an abyss of cold gray mist, driven ever and anon like showers of hail into your face, as you grope your way down the rocky slope. Haste not, pause not. Here is the platform, half-seen, half-felt amid the blinding spray. Shade of Father Hennepin, this is truly a 'dismal roaring' of wind and water. We are across —and stand secure on the smooth shaly bottom of the cave. Look up! what a magnificent arch is formed by the solid rock on the one side, and the descending mass of water on the other. Which is the solider and firmer you hardly know. Yet look again—for it is sunset—and see what we shall see nowhere else on earth, three rainbows one within another, not half-formed and incomplete, as is the scheme of our daily life; but filling up the complete circle, perfect and absolute."

THE ROCK OF AGES is the huge rock lying at the foot of the Falls in front of the Cave of the Winds.

From the foot of the staircase, the path to the left, leads toward the Horse-Shoe Fall. Portions of the rock fall occasionally, and the road is but little used, and not kept in good condition; still, one is well repaid for an attempt to get a close sight of the Great Fall from below. Returning to the bank above, and continuing the walk along the brink, the next interesting point of observation is

TERRAPIN BRIDGE, leading to the edge of the Horse-Shoe Fall and the TERRAPIN ROCK, where for forty years the well-known TERRAPIN TOWER, standing at the very verge of the Falls, constituted a land-mark to be seen from all directions. The bridge, being so near the Fall as to be affected by the spray, requires that those who pass over it should avoid exposure. The water at this extremity of the Fall descends in light feathery foam, contrasting finely with the solid masses in which it seems to plunge down the center of the sweeping curve. The line of division between the government of the United States and that of Canada is in the deepest part of the channel, or through the angular part of the Fall. It passes through the lonely little GULL ISLAND in the center of the river, which has never been trodden by human foot.

Following a road along the south side of the Island, affording an unsurpassed view of the Canadian Rapids, which run at the rate of 28 miles per hour, we come to the

THREE SISTERS ISLANDS, connected with Goat Island and with one another by three beautiful bridges. Their location in the mist of the Rapids afford many varied and desirable points to observe the scenery. From the head of the Third Sister a continuous cascade extending toward the Canada shore as far as the eye can reach, and from which the spray rises in beautiful clouds, presents a peculiar phenomenon usually termed the

LEAPING ROCK—doubtlessly a misnomer. The water striking against the rock rises perpetually in an unbroken column, twenty or more feet high, producing a brilliant effect.

THE HERMIT'S CASCADE is spanned by the First Sister Island Bridge, and is a rare and attractive Fall. It was one of the favorite resorts of the Hermit of the Falls.

AT THE HEAD OF GOAT ISLAND, a little further up the river, the view is quite expansive, commanding both banks of the stream, and the islands in the channel. Beginning at the right, the site of Fort Schlosser is seen about a mile away, marked by a small white building and a very large chimney. The town of Chippewa on the Canada shore; Grand Island, etc., are all visible from this point.

We leave with reluctance this most fascinating spot, and direct our steps towards the Canada Side, crossing the river this time over

THE NEW SUSPENSION BRIDGE, in full view of the Great Cataract, from which one of the most glorious views of the entire Falls can be had.

The points already visited constitute the attractions immediately around the Falls. There are several localities in the vicinity worthy of attention, specially on account of historical associations. A brief mention will aid the tourist in his peregrinations.

THE MICHIGAN CENTRAL CANTI-LEVER BRIDGE, just constructed, a structure of an entirely new model and positively elegant.

THE OLD SUSPENSION BRIDGE two miles below the Falls. This was built in 1855 by John A. Roebling, and is both a railroad and carriage bridge. It is a marvel of engineering some 8,000 miles of wire being employed in the cables.

WHIRLPOOL RAPIDS.—The narrowing of the channel in the vicinity of the Suspension Bridge greatly accelerates the current, and the tremendous force with which it rushes through the gorge throws the water into violent commotion. On the American side a double elevator, and on the Canada side an inclined railway have been provided to descend to the water's edge and take a near view of the wild scene.

THE WHIRLPOOL.—A half mile below the Rapids, the Whirlpool is found. Here the river makes an acute angle in its course, turning to the right, and boils within a narrower compass than in any other spot. The current of the river runs with such fierce velocity, that it rises up in the middle ten to twenty feet above the sides. On the surface of this whirling vortex are often seen the ruins of forest floating round, marking out to the eye the outline of that fatal circle. The Whirlpool may be seen to advantage from either the Canadian or the American side.

THE MANITOU, OR PINNACLE ROCK, is supposed to be a portion of the cliff, at the base of which it lies, thrown down in former times. It is situated about fifty rods above the Whirlpool, at the edge of the river, its shape being that of an inverted cone, with its apex resting upon the summit of another large rock, reaching to the height of nearly one hundred feet from the water's edge.

BROCK'S MONUMENT.—On Queenston Heights, four miles below the Whirlpool, on the Canada side, stands the Monument erected to the memory of the British General, Sir Isaac Brock, who fell in the sanguinary action fought on the spot on the 15th of October, 1812. The view from this monument is most gorgeous. The eye wanders with untiring delight over a rich scene of woodland and water. Just below, is the village of QUEENSTON, ONTARIO, a small picturesque town, worth of notice chiefly on account of the memorable battle that took place on the neighboring heights.

LEWISTON, N. Y., opposite Queenston, is a beautifully situated town, about seven miles from the Falls. It is a place of some importance, and stands at the head of the navigation on the river; it contains several fine hotels and public buildings.

NIAGARA TOWN stands on the Canada shore, opposite Youngstown, on the site of Newark, which was burnt in 1813 by General McClure. A short distance above the town are the remains of FORT GEORGE, which was taken by the Americans in 1813, afterward destroyed by the British and left in ruins.

FORT NIAGARA stands at the mouth of the Niagara River on the American side. There are many interesting associations connected with this spot. During the earlier part of the past century, it was the scene of many severe conflicts between the whites and the indians, and subsequently between the English and the French. It was established as a trading post by La Salle in 1678. The village adjacent to the Fort is called YOUNGS- TOWN, in honor of its founder, the late John Young, Esq.

FORT MISSASAUGA, also at the mouth of the river, opposite Fort Niagara, is a little below the town of Niagara, and is garrisoned by British soldiers.

THE DEVIL'S HOLE, on the American side, three miles below the Falls, is a large chasm in the bank of the river, which receives the water from a small stream known as Bloody Run; it was the scene of the murder of the English, 600 in number, by the French and Indians in 1793, when only three of the number escaped to tell the tale.

LUNDY'S LANE BATTLE GROUND located one and one-half miles west of the Falls, was the scene of a sanguinary action between the British and American forces, on July 25th, 1814, the loss on both sides in killed and wounded being 1,800.

DRUMMONDVILLE, in the immediate vicinity, is named after General Drummond, then commander of the British forces.

CHIPPEWA BATTLE GROUND.—Upon this field, located near the village on the Canada bank of the Niagara, three miles above the Falls, was fought the first of that series of actions which decided the campaign of 1814 in favor of the American arms. The battle took place on July 5th, 1814. The British made the attack and retreated after the action.

THE TOP OF THE MOUNTAIN, on the American side, opposite Queenston Heights, affords from its elevated position a magnificent view of Lake Ontario and the River Niagara.

THE TUSCARORA INDIAN RESERVATION is 9 miles northeast from the Falls. It is strictly an Indian village upon which the Tuscaroras are located, and well worth a visit.

As a parting injunction to the visitors of the future, the pilgrim would advise them, *invariably*, to make distinct agreements with the hackmen or any other person whose services they may require at Niagara Falls, as to the service expected and the amount to be paid in return. Exact the terms of your contract, but do not go beyond without first having a thorough understanding as to the cost.

www.ingramcontent.com/pod-product-compliance
Lightning Source LLC
Chambersburg PA
CBHW030310170426
43202CB00009B/941